Waldemar Sch

from
MBA
to
CEO

THE JOB OF THE CEO AND HOW YOU GET IT

Editora Val de Mar

From MBA to CEO

The Job of the CEO and how you get it

Book design: The Author & Marianne Gulstad, Publizon
Printed by CreateSpace, An Amazon.com Company

1st edition 2013
ISBN 978-2-9700884-0-0

Published by Editora Val de Mar
Email address: CEO@editoravaldemar.com

FOREWORD BY
DAMIEN O'BRIEN

CEO & CHAIRMAN OF EGON ZEHNDER

From MBA to CEO is a very special career book because the author is a practitioner: Waldemar Schmidt, who has been CEO of a very large global group, chairman of several global companies and a noted lecturer on business education.

The single most frequent question that MBA students raised to the author during his numerous lectures was "How do I become a CEO?" Not alone does *From MBA to CEO* answer this question. It also addresses a wide range of career issues that MBA students from ten of the world's leading business schools raised in a research project conducted by the author. And it tackles matters that students have not yet realised might affect them.

From MBA to CEO is a unique and tailor-made career guide for MBA graduates and other men and women with CEO dreams. The book gives insights into the job of the CEO, it helps readers assess whether they have what it takes to become a CEO, what they must endure and achieve and how to progress all the way to the top. "How to work with search firms" is a very special chapter that gives readers invaluable advice that could have significant influence on their careers.

Our firm, Egon Zehnder, has helped the author over several decades to recruit and assess leaders around the globe. We are pleased to have been involved in the *MBA to CEO* project. We believe that this book constitutes a unique how-to tool for ambitious men and women who dream of becoming CEOs.

Damien O'Brien
MBA Graduate from Columbia University
CEO & Chairman of Egon Zehnder

TO MBAs

WHO STRIVE TO BECOME GREAT

LEADERS IN ORDER TO ACHIEVE

THEIR DREAM OF BECOMING

SUCCESSFUL CEOs

CONTENTS

PART IV
CAREER PLANNING AND EXECUTION
—A LIFELONG TASK

PART V
HOW TO DEAL WITH
CRITICAL CAREER AND LEADERSHIP ISSUES

PART VI
BACKSTAGE INFORMATION

INTRODUCTION

If your dream is to become a CEO, you must keep *From MBA to CEO* by your side throughout your career.

From MBA to CEO is about *inspiring* and *guiding* young men and women throughout their careers to become great leaders in order to help them become successful CEOs.

Every question that you have cannot be answered in this book, but I can inspire you to plan, to reflect and to use sound judgement throughout your career.

It is perhaps easier to get the job of CEO than it is to keep it; therefore, we have set out to inspire you to behave in such a manner that you will help you to retain this job.

I am an experienced global CEO and Chairman who has taught leadership to MBA students at IMD, LBS and CBS. For the writing of this book, I teamed up with Egon Zehnder, a leading global search firm, and about 200 MBA students from some of the world's preeminent business school, thus enabling myself, as the author, to provide the very best insight, expertise and advice available.

The reason for writing this book was simple: during the course of my lectures and career, I was asked a tremendous amount of questions about how to become a CEO. This book was the obvious way of making these views, observations and personal experiences of the topic available to all MBAs who dream of becoming successful CEOs.

The objective has been to write a book that will become the MBA's primary reference and career guide for their entire professional life.

We cover all sizes of CEO jobs, from small businesses to very large ones.

Importantly, however, we don't believe that we can teach people to become great leaders, but we *do* believe that we can *inspire* people to become great leaders. We also believe that you must be a great leader if your dream is to become a successful CEO. Being a successful CEO is very much about skills and mindset.

We have conducted a research project with the aim of identifying the most pressing questions of ambitious MBA students with CEO ambitions, as well as addressing such questions. We have also incorporated issues that were not raised during our sessions but which we know, from experience, that people with CEO ambitions encounter during their careers. We address all of these topics and give our best advice and guidance to each of them.

HOW TO READ THE BOOK:

The book is designed in a manner that will help you to achieve your career goals. It should be on your iPad and by your bedside throughout your entire career. When you dive into the book for the first time, we recommend you read it in chronological order. If you do so, you will find that it contains some repetition: this is deliberate so that thereafter you can dive into the chapters you need.

THE BOOK IS STRUCTURED AS FOLLOWS:

- **MY OWN STORY, 'FROM LOCAL BOY TO GLOBAL CEO'**: Progressing through my own story in detail has helped me to understand the issues faced by young professionals with CEO ambitions. It has also helped me to conclude that CEOs are not born but are made when given opportunities and taking the chance to utilise such opportunities.

- **PART I** provides practical and deep insights into the role of CEO.

- **PART II** explains the characteristics and skills of great leaders.

- **PART III** is centred on reflection, and self-assessing your determination and leadership potential to become a CEO. We help you establish whether or not you really want to become a CEO, and if you have what it takes to become a successful CEO.

- **PART IV** is concerned with career planning. Subjects covered include how to leverage your MBA, how to make a career plan, the creation of a personal brand, stepping onto the career ladder, how to climb the career ladder, and how to work with executive search firms.

- **PART V** is about many of the career and leadership issues that you will encounter throughout you career. Some of the issues were discovered during our research project.

Others fall into the category, 'You don't know what you don't know'. These are issues that we have come across during our many years of experience in business. You can also see this last part of the book as an easy way of getting inspiration regarding issues covered in the book, as well as about issues *not* covered elsewhere in the book.

ABOUT OUR RESEARCH:

Our research project very much supports the view that there is a real and unmet need for our book. The participating students we spoke to during the course of the research phase said that they were unable to find books that could help them with their career all the way from the Classroom to the Boardroom.

We interacted with approximately 200 MBA students from ten of the world's leading business schools. Half accepted our invitation to have their names mentioned in the book. Between them, they represent more than 50 nationalities from all five continents.

We have been overwhelmed by students' interest in the topic of how to become a successful CEO. This interest was evidenced by audience responses to a lecture entitled, 'The Job of CEO and How You Get It', which was devised and delivered at the participating schools.

We conducted a qualitative research amongst 200 MBA students, and held career and leadership sessions with many of them, during which time they helped us to define their key questions. We received more than 1,000 questions during the course of the study, posed by the MBA students. Many questions raised the same concerns, and we took this into account when structuring the book.

Many of the students also had access to early drafts of the book and contributed with a wealth of valuable insight. Thus, the book is a result of a fantastic collaborative effort between the book team and students from the participating business schools.

MY HOPE: Normally I do not apply 'MBH—Management By Hope'—but in this case I do: it is my sincere hope that *From MBA to CEO*, with its wealth of advice will *inspire* and *guide* young men and women to become great leaders—and, subsequently, successful CEOs.

It is also my hope that young executives with degrees other than an MBA will be inspired by the book and thus achieve their own career goals.

THANK YOU: As great leaders know, a one-person team can only achieve very limited results in business, and the same applies when writing books. I am therefore very grateful to have been able to work with a fantastic team and book community. A big thank you goes to Egon Zehnder, to the participating business schools and their busy and enthusiastic students, to Clare MacCarthy for editorial advice, and to our sponsor—the Apax Foundation.

Waldemar Schmidt

FROM LOCAL BOY
TO GLOBAL CEO

It was only after I stepped down from my job as Group Chief Executive of ISS, having held management and CEO positions for over 35 years, that I first began to explore underlying issues of leadership, its fundamental nature, and the mechanisms involved. I became very interested in career development when I started lecturing about leadership to MBA students at the International Institute for Management Development in Lausanne (IMD), London Business School (LBS) and Copenhagen Business School (CBS).

Stepping down from a very hectic and demanding CEO role and then taking on the role of Chairman in many companies really opened my eyes. During my time as Executive in Residence at IMD—during which time I wrote *Winning at Service—Lessons from Service Leaders*—and lectured on Leadership for MBA classes, I trawled through the subject of leadership.

Amongst the first things I did when I decided to write *From MBA to CEO* was, for the first time ever, casting a glance backwards over my life to see how an ordinary boy from Haderslev, a small town in provincial Denmark, was given opportunities that ultimately led to acquiring the role of CEO of a global company with 250,000 employees. I have tried very hard and objectively to analyse the opportunities that I have been given and the choices I have made. I have also looked back at lessons learnt.

We decided to include my story in the book because we believe that this true life narrative includes lessons, experiences and key decisions that can inspire aspiring CEOs throughout their entire careers.

It was not written in the stars that I was going to rise to such a major role. As mentioned previously, I was a very ordinary middle-class boy from a small town in Denmark.

If you were to ask my teachers and childhood friends, I do not believe any of them would have predicted I would become CEO of a major global company. The only small leadership roles I had in my early years were as a patrol leader with the boy scouts and later as Deputy Chairman of the Young Conservatives Club in my home town—though, in complete honesty, I cannot recall deriving any significant leadership lessons from either position.

I still recall a very special experience that I had during a Young Conservatives Board meeting in a hotel in my hometown. A guest at a neighbouring table became interested in what we were doing. He turned out to be a Swedish engineer who had lived and worked in the US for Ericsson, and was on his way back to Sweden in his big American car. He asked each of us in turn, starting with myself, what kind of job we had and about our career plans. I told him that I was going to study engineering, upon which he pulled out from his pocket a US silver dollar. He gave it to me with the words, 'This is to remind you that you should go for a post-grad at MIT'. I still have that very same silver dollar but, as things transpired, I never had the spare time necessary between jobs to pursue a post-grad study.

As a boy, I wanted to be a medical doctor. The sight of our family doctor's car—a splendid white Ford cabriolet with a powerful V8 engine—perhaps inspired this ambition. An American beauty such as this was a rare sight in my country in the aftermath of the Second World War. However, as I grew older, I realised that the study of medicine was almost perpetual. By the time I reached the age of fifteen, I was very tired of going to school. I was quite proficient at maths, had a good pair of hands, and was very interested in technical matters. One of my father's friends was an engineer who had his own company producing agricultural machines. I was invited to visit the factory and immediately **decided** I wanted to become a mechanical engineer with a degree based on apprenticeship and a bachelor's degree.

My key lesson from my four years as an apprentice—repairing ploughs, tractors and combine harvesters—was a deep respect for people on the floor and their pride in doing a good job. I also benefitted from hands-on manual work. Work discipline was another key lesson from my period on the 'workshop floor'. We worked a nine-hour day, starting at 07:30, and had a great deal of overtime during the high season, which lasted from the spring until late-summer, when the harvest was completed. A long day in the repair workshop concluded with a bicycle ride home as I had no car during my time as an apprentice.

At engineering school, I did not get involved in student organisation. After the first year, I made a **decision** that greatly influenced my career: I **decided** to specialise in industrial engineering as I could not see myself at a drawing Board in an engineering company designing valves or some such.

As a student, I kept a scrapbook. The front cover bore a photograph of an E-type Jaguar with my handwritten comment underneath, 'Therefore!' This was a memo to self-remind me that the hard grind of studying one day would reward me sufficiently to enable the purchase of this dream car.

9

Meanwhile, I benefitted immensely from taking courses in accounting, cost calculation and English. However, one crucial component was absent from my studies—management. It simply wasn't taught. And although I had not formulated my career plans and prospects, I felt that management would play a key role in my professional life.

The key lessons from my engineering studies have proven to be an important base for my early jobs. I learnt how to plan, as well as the importance of planning. In addition, I learnt how to organise and how to control. Coincidentally, these are the most important elements of Peter Drucker's definition of management.

As graduation time drew closer, I made another **decision** that moved me further from the usual engineering career track. I had looked at a number of traditional industrial engineering jobs involving production planning, time and motion studies, etc. in premier manufacturing companies in Denmark but found nothing that gripped my attention. As such, I broadened my scope and soon hit upon an intriguing opportunity: a young and fast-growing Danish company called Dansk Chrysanthemum Kultur (DCK) with production facilities on the Italian island of Sardinia and headquarters in Denmark. Though only established four years beforehand, DCK was already Europe's largest industrial nursery and producer of flower cuttings, including chrysanthemums and carnations, for example. The company advertised a job for an industrial engineer for its production-planning department at its headquarters near Copenhagen.

The interview I had with the general manager, Jens Andersen, which took place one Saturday morning, remains crystal clear in my mind. Towards the end of the time allotted, a tall and captivating individual entered the room and listened intently to our conversation for approximately ten minutes, after which time he left with a polite nod. Two minutes later, the telephone rang and Jens Andersen just repeated a single word 'Yes' three or four times. Putting down the receiver, he told me that the person on the phone was the 'silent visitor' who had just left the room—the company's CEO and founder, Jan Bonde Nielsen.

The message from the CEO—who, at 26, was just two years older than me—was clear: I could start on Monday, two days later. As DCK and the role proposed felt so right for me, this was welcome news.

I was over the moon: I had found a dream job—and it was very well paid. I travelled back home with a signed contract. I actually only started my new job 9 days later since I still had one subject left in my graduation exam.

I started out with the job I was hired to do—production planning at the company's headquarters, an old farmhouse near Copenhagen. From the outset, I worked very hard and put in long hours. Six months later, however, I was transferred to the production facilities near a beautiful beach on the island of Sardinia along with a group of young colleagues. I had just celebrated my 25th birthday when I travelled from Copenhagen Airport to Cagliari Airport, Sardinia, on a cargo DC-6 with my colleagues, a few personal belongings and, as I remember it, a small tractor for the nursery. This was my very first flight, and I was on my way to an exciting future.

I stayed with DCK for four years, and was continually given new positions with management responsibility for production, maintenance and construction, logistics, and project management. I do not quite know why and how I moved from one position to another, but this hardly mattered: it was a terrific way to kick off a career. The company grew at an impressive pace, engendering a dynamic work environment with plenty of opportunities to take on new tasks; great young colleagues from many different countries, in a foreign country, a different culture, and a new language to be learnt. The advantages were numerous.

An ancillary benefit for a motor enthusiast such as me was the opportunity to progress up the car ownership ladder. During my short stint at DCK HQ in Denmark I had bought my first car, which was a white Volkswagen Beetle. Though an iconic model in many respects, the only resemblance it bore to the Ford cabriolet of my youth was its colour and sunroof. In Italy, I upgraded to a white Fiat 850 Spider, a small but beautifully formed convertible designed by the great Giuseppe Bertone. Although still a long way from the Jaguar E-type of my dreams, the Spider was perfect for a bachelor in sunny Sardinia.

After my four fantastic years in Sardinia, I again made a very conscious **decision**, which influenced my life and career in a big way: I quit my wonderful job in Italy because I had become very interested in Mr Bonde Nielsen's PA at the HQ in Copenhagen— Britta Hansson. I left my dream job in sunny Italy and moved back to Copenhagen without having a new job. My first priority was not a new job but, at this point in my life, a young lady.

My key learnings in Italy can be summed up as follows:

- A new ability to manage and work alongside people of many cultures and languages on foreign soil in a fast-growing business.

- A new language—Italian—and I had my first and very valuable experience of having responsibility for people and budgets.

- If you show initiative and work hard, opportunities come your way. You learn a tremendous amount by having many different jobs in the same company.

12

It was not without regret that I said goodbye to my sunny Mediterranean island. Although I had not had any formal profit and loss responsibility, I believed that I had reaped a wealth of experience from my Sardinian sojourn. I had my priorities straight and I realised that hard work and dedication were good for your career.

Back in Denmark, I was very lucky to get the girlfriend who had prompted my **decision** to return, and I had a very clear idea about the kind of job I wanted to have next. I wanted an expatriate job with a large, global Danish company. I had two companies in my sights: EAC—The East Asiatic Company—which, at the time, was one of the largest companies in Scandinavia and a very prestigious employer, and which, at that point in time, was a shipping, trading and industrial conglomerate; the other company on my list was FLS, a world leader in building cement factories around the world. I sought the advice of my boss, Jan Bonde Nielsen, who was very clear that I should go for a role at EAC as he believed I was more of a businessman than an engineer. This was good advice and in line with my own conclusions.

By coincidence, I saw an advertisement in a Danish newspaper, detailing EAC's search for an engineer for its industrial department at the HQ in Copenhagen. This department looked after more than 100 industrial companies around the globe. However, the job advertised was not the kind of job I wanted—nor was I qualified for it. Furthermore, it was based in Copenhagen. My dream was to be posted to Asia. However, as EAC rarely recruited engineers, I wanted to use this opportunity to get my foot in the door. They had a culture of only employing trainees straight from school and not of recruiting from the outside. Traditionally, chairmen, CEOs, executive committee members, country managers were all Danes who had started as trainees in EAC. I responded to the ad and was invited in for an interview. The first part of the interview was in the HR Department. I filled in the obligatory application form and went through a fairly standard interview; however, I do remember vividly that one of the questions on the form was something along the lines of, 'Why would you like an overseas posting?' My answer was clear: 'Because I think I will be able to get a management role at a younger age than if I remain in Denmark'. Upon reflection, I feel that my answer to this question has been extremely significant to the way in which my professional life panned out subsequently. The second part comprised an interview with Mr Otto Feierskov Andreasen, during which we had a great conversation. He was a very likable person, and I only realised that he was Deputy Managing Director when I looked at his business card post-interview. A few days afterwards, I received a contract to work as a management trainee at HQ in Copenhagen for 12 months, after which I would be posted to one of EAC's overseas industrial companies.

Although my time at EAC's head office in Copenhagen turned out to be rather shorter than anticipated originally, I nevertheless made several useful insights—not least of these was a deeper understanding of the workings of a head office, and of what was expected of the subsidiaries and their general managers.

I was, at this stage, back in Denmark, had a lovely girlfriend and a job with great overseas career potential. Expecting to stay at home for a year or so, I replaced my Italian Spider 850 with a classic red MGB roadster. As another cabriolet, it was inappropriate for the Danish climate but was wonderful to drive.

Then, quite out of the blue and just three months into the planned 12-month management trainee period, opportunity knocked: it was decided that I would be transferred to São Paulo, Brazil as General Manager (the CEO term was not used at this time) of a start-up company. The company was called Kemiform and specialised in the manufacturing of components for the electronics industry with a unique photochemical process. The prospect of becoming a General Manager at the age of 29 easily overcame my preference to avoid manufacturing industries. Nevertheless, I had one very serious issue to resolve before I would say 'yes' to going to Brazil: my girlfriend. In those days, the company dictated that you could not bring your girlfriend with you on overseas postings—but you could bring your wife. This was therefore a great opportunity to ask my girlfriend and ex-colleague if she would marry me. Fortunately, the answer was yes. Funnily enough, I also had to formally ask the EAC to agree to my marriage. During the next months, I spent most of my time at Kemiform in Denmark learning everything about their technology processes, cost calculations, sales and marketing, administration, etc. Eight months into my 12-month contract as a management trainee, again, my life changed in a very significant way. I had married the girl I had dreamt about since my years in Italy, and I would become a general manager in a foreign country. Leaving Denmark on a snowy November day, we headed for sunny São Paulo and an incredible ten-year 'honeymoon trip' to a fantastic new country.

My new role was a classic start-up experience: I had to hire a team, train the new workers, set up the factory and find customers. My business card read *gerente geral* (general manager)—a minor role of CEO in today's terminology. I did not have a business card in my first job so now having one with the title of General Manager (CEO) felt really good. It felt great to be a general manager at 29 years of age with responsibility for 'everything'.

Over the next three years at Kemiform, we had a wonderful time. I hired and trained some great managers and staff to join our pioneering start-up company. It was a very hands-on management task in a company with only around 20 employees. Kemiform developed very well, made profits after 18 months, and I learnt an awful lot during this time. My key learnings can be summarised as full profit and loss responsibility, and everything that came with a general management position, namely strategy, budgets, execution, people and customers. In addition, I definitely learnt a lot about business-to-business sales by visiting more than 1,500 potential customers, explaining the technical advantages of our new technology and winning business. I also managed to become just about as a fluent in the Portuguese language as a foreigner can become.

During this period, I also received my first company car—another white VW Beetle. Though it had no air conditioning, no sunroof and had beige plastic seats, it was still my first company car. It wasn't flash but it served me well in a job that required sales visits to more than 1,500 potential customers in Greater São Paulo. My wife and I also explored as much of Brazil as we could in the Beetle.

After my first three years in Brazil as general manager of Kemiform, I was asked to carry out a feasibility and market study for the industrial department of EAC. The project was to look at the market for contract cleaning—the daily cleaning of offices, factories, hospitals, airports, etc. The EAC had entered a joint venture agreement with a Danish company called ISS—a European leader in the contract cleaning industry. The idea was to combine EAC's local know-how with ISS's industry expertise by setting up overseas 50/50 joint ventures in this particular service industry. ISS wanted to expand outside of Europe but needed a partner with local business knowledge.

Contract cleaning was an industry about which I knew nothing and I had never heard of ISS. Nevertheless, I got hold of the Yellow Pages in São Paulo with the aim of identifying the major players in the contract cleaning business on a local scale. This led to a whole range of meetings, including with the owners of the five largest players in the industry in São Paulo. All of these five company owners were open to talks about selling their companies. I prepared a feasibility report containing my recommendations to EAC in Copenhagen. After discussions between EAC and ISS, ISS's Business Development Director, Ib Goldschmidt, came to Brazil for two weeks with the objective and mandate to acquire one of the five companies. Ib Goldschmidt and I visited them all, and we quickly identified a clear preference for one particular company, Limpadora Continental. By the end of Ib Goldschmidt's two-week visit, we had signed a letter of intent with our favourite candidate. However, well before this, Ib Goldschmidt had told me that I was going to become Managing Director (CEO) of the company that we were going to acquire. I did not like the idea of working in the contract cleaning industry, which I found very primitive in Brazil. It also seemed a step too far away from my engineering degree, and I therefore, very politely but also firmly, declined the offer. However, Ib Goldschmidt pressed on to change my mind by talking about ISS and how it had professionalised the industry in Scandinavia. He also pointed out that the ISS group CEO, Poul Andreassen, as well as some of the group's senior executives, were industrial engineers. ISS was an acronym for International Service System. The word system referred to the industrial engineering business approach that ISS had adopted. During Ib Goldschmidt's second weekend in Brazil—which he spent together with my wife and I in our home—we had both fallen for his salesmanship. He recognised this and asked me again. I **decided** to say 'yes, thank you'. This proved to be yet another **decision** that changed the rest of my professional life in a big way—and one that also influenced our family life—big time. ISS became part of my life and, to a great degree, a part of my family's life. With the new job as Country Manager for ISS in Brazil, I stepped up from General Manager to Managing Director, and moved away from manufacturing to a very labour-intensive service industry.

After having signed the deal to acquire one of the five companies, I travelled to Copenhagen, where I spent a fascinating month learning 'everything about contract cleaning and service management'. I worked as a cleaner between five and eight in the morning at the Technical University of Denmark in order to learn about the job on the floor; in effect, a 'post-grad' in the practicalities of cleaning. I spent the rest of the working day (and more) at HQ, meeting people and learning what I needed to know about all key functions in the business.

After my training, I went back to Brazil and took over my new job as Managing Director/Country Manager of one Brazil's largest companies in the industry. The company had 1,200 employees—a huge step up from 20 employees in Kemiform. I was 32 years old at the time, and had realised my dream of getting an important management job at a young age. You can only imagine how proud I felt when I received my business card with the title *Diretor Gerente* (Managing Director). Importantly, I don't believe I would have become CEO of a company with 1,200 employees at the age of 32 had I remained in Denmark.

With a bigger job came a bigger car; first an Opala Chevrolet and then a more sporty Alfa Romeo 2300ti. Both cars' hard 4-cylinder engines were manufactured in Brazil and were based on dated European models. They bore little resemblance to the Jaguar E-type but were better than the Beetle.

I still remember the incredible weight of responsibility I felt on May 2, 1973 when I entered the door to my new company. How could little me be Managing Director of such a large company? Strangely enough, I never had the same feeling in my subsequent career progression at ISS—not even when I became Group CEO 22 years later. It was an incredible feeling. But I very quickly got into the new job.

My first priority was to recruit a management team, with whom I would develop a shared vision. I found two fantastic colleagues, Robert Brendim as Operations Manager and

Roslavo Noguiera Lima as Financial Manager. The vision we developed was very simple: we wanted to be the industry leader in all aspects: professionalism, growth and profitability. Whereas many Country Managers try to minimise interactions with HQ, we decided to get a lot of assistance from some of the outstanding specialists from HQ. They came out for periods of 1–2 months in order to help train and develop local talent. We did not believe that having a lot of expatriates in the company was necessary as we were able to attract many young, talented and hard-working Brazilians to join us. One of the things of which I am most proud has been to see so many of my colleagues grow with the company. As an example, Rosalvo progressed from Finance Manager to Country Manager long after I left Brazil. Things went very well for us. We drew attention at HQ and we evolved into very special company in the ISS family. However, there were constant problems to overcome; high rates of inflation, poorly educated workers, changing legislation, to name but a few. It was our strategy to focus on mainly large multinational companies as our customers. This taught us to focus on the quality of our services, which helped us to become industry leaders to the extent that our competitors poached people from us and tried to copy many of the things we did. I am very proud when people in the industry say that we, at ISS, raised the standards of the whole industry in Brazil.

For me personally, it was an unbelievable experience to get the opportunity to manage a large and fast-growing company in a very dynamic market so far away from home.

After a decade in Brazil—of which seven years were spent as Managing Director of ISS in Brazil—I made another big **decision** that was supported by my wife. This was, once again, a move that was very important for my professional life—and certainly for my family life. I **decided** that I wanted to go back to live and work in Denmark. We enjoyed Brazil a lot, and there was more to do in the job that I loved. We had a very pleasant lifestyle with many friends plus a large house, pool, servants, membership of Clube de Campo in São Paulo, subtropical climate and much more. Brazil and its people are something you need to have experienced to understand fully the excitement and joy. Somehow, however, we felt we should not spend the rest of our lives there.

I informed my Board of our decision very early on so that we could prepare for an orderly succession, and I told both shareholders that I would start looking for a new job in Denmark and that I had one very attractive possibility. I felt that joining one of the two partners would cause problems with the other; however, both offered me a job. I accepted the job that ISS offered me as I identified with the company and its values, and I knew the business from the ground. My successor, who chose a title that I very much dislike (*Diretor Presidente*) was recruited, and I was ready for a big move.

My key learning in Brazil can be summed up as follows:

- **KEMIFORM**: As General Manager, I had full responsibility for the strategy of the company, for profit and loss (P&L), for a small management team, and hands-on involvement in production, sales and finance. I had the experience of starting up a company from scratch far away from home, and I learnt to work in a hierarchy through a Country Manager to the Head Office 10,000 kilometres away. Getting my first CEO job at an early age has been crucial for my career.

- **ISS**: The progression from General Manager to Managing Director meant reporting to a Board for the first time in my career. This taught me the importance of preparing and structuring Board meetings diligently and cleverly in order to enhance my chances of the acceptance of my ideas and proposals. I learnt the importance of employing people with great potential and how to let them get on with the job and to grow with the company. The company we acquired was a family-owned company started by a very clever Portuguese immigrant, Orlando Barreira Palmas. We successfully professionalised the company to the extent that we also professionalised the whole industry. I learnt about the importance of having a clear strategy: not to be everything to everybody. We made a deliberate choice to focus on multinational customers who wanted high standards of quality despite an inherent lack of well-trained manpower. This job was a real CEO role, with full responsibility for 'everything'.

- **BRAZIL**: I cannot over-emphasise how exciting and career-enhancing my ten years (1969–1979) in Brazil have been for myself and the rest of the Schmidt family. Brazil gets into your blood because of its people! I agree with those who say that you become 'tropicalised' in Brazil. I certainly came back to Europe a very different person, and I am certain that my ten-year experience in Brazil has been the event that has shaped my career most predominantly.

I returned to Denmark and became Executive Vice President as head of Europe and Brazil, and a member of the group's Management Board. I believed that it was a dream job—although not a CEO job with responsibility for 'everything'. The management of EAC agreed to my move, although I was originally their man. Indeed, EAC was gracious enough to say that having me at ISS would be positive for the on-going cooperation between the two groups.

I moved back to Denmark with a truckload of fantastic experiences and memories: a 10-year honeymoon period with my wife, two children born in Brazil, and a third child made in Brazil to be born in Denmark four months after our return. Added to this was some solid career experience that had opened the door for a dream job in one of Denmark's largest and most keenly watched companies. I was 39 years old at the time—an age that suited the job.

I learnt quickly that the change from being 'King in Brazil' to being 'Prince in Denmark' was very difficult and often very frustrating. Being 10,000 kilometres away from your boss is very different from having him on the floor just above you. What is more, moving to HQ is not easy unless you become the group CEO. In fact, it was a major chock to my system.

From time to time, executive search firms, CEOs and chairmen approached me with job offers. However, with one exception, I believed that the grass was probably not any greener in another company. I always discussed these issues with my wife, and she unfailingly supported me when I **decided** to stay put. The only job opportunity to which I felt attracted was a CEO position in a mid-sized publicly listed company in Denmark. One of their Board members encouraged me to apply for the job, which I did. I liked the company, and related very well to the chairman and all Board members except one, who was opposed to my appointment, thus meaning I did not get the job. With hindsight, I should be very grateful that this man did not think I was the right person for the job as getting that job would have led to a very different career for me. My move would have been a 'double switch', i.e. from EVP to CEO, and in a completely different industry. I did not know the term 'double switch' at the time, and seemingly did not get my risk assessment right.

This particular company no longer exists—and so I should be thankful that someone else made this crucial **decision** for me.

My 10 years as Executive Vice President at headquarters gave me a series of insights that stood me in good stead in years to come:

1. I came to the conclusion that HQ should be small and be the architect of strategy, the allocation of financial resources and financial control. Operations should be left to operators.

2. It is good for your career to spend some shorter periods at HQ in order to stay in touch and to be visible to the CEO and Board.

3. If you spend too long a period at HQ, as EVP or similar, you risk becoming labelled as a 'Number Two' man or woman, and therefore are unsuitable for the top job.

4. The job as EVP is far less independent than the job as Country or Regional CEO away from HQ.

Of course, my tenure at the ISS headquarters also offered new motoring experiences. The best company car to which I was entitled was the Audi 100 (now the Audi 6). I had three of these in a row and enjoyed the top-quality German build—a huge improvement on what I was used to in Brazil. Moreover, I couldn't help but think that Audi's famous company slogan *Vorsprung durch Technik* (progress through technology) was also a fitting metaphor for my own progression through car ownership!

My work situation became much better when my boss decided to even further decentralise operations at ISS. On a trip with him to Germany, he very surprisingly asked me if I would move to London to do my job from there. He was in doubt because he thought that our **decision** to move back from Brazil meant that my wife and I had decided to stay in Denmark for good. I told him that it sounded very attractive indeed and that I would get back to him the next day after talking with my wife. When I came back home from the trip to Germany late in the evening, my wife and I only needed a quick drink and a very short conversation before we agreed that moving to London would be great job- and family-wise. We agreed that it would be a fantastic experience for our three young children: the same company and the same job but away from the boss. Absolutely ideal.

I became Managing Director (CEO) of ISS Europe Limited, which also included operations in Brazil and, later, Asia. It was incredibly wonderful to have a CEO role again! Furthermore, I continued to be a member of the group's Executive Management Board and therefore participated in all group Bard meetings in Copenhagen.

So, after 10 years at HQ, we again moved away from Denmark. I built up a small organisation in London with a great team. I was 49 years old and did not at all aspire to succeeding my boss as Group CEO. I agreed with the Board that I would remain in the job in London for the next 16 years until my retirement.

My company car in London was a Jaguar XJ with an 8-cylinder engine. It wasn't the E-type but it was a Jaguar.

Being away from HQ and having the independence that this provided meant that things quickly started to go very well for us. We grew the business organically and through acquisitions. Profitability increased and we developed and focused the strategy of our part of the group. In addition, we acquired the largest Asian competitor, which then became part of ISS Europe and Brazil.

Based on my results, my boss started to ask if I would be prepared to return to Copenhagen to take over his job as CEO of the group. For quite some time I got away with politely saying that I was very happy in London, as was my family. However, after a Board meeting in Geneva, he suggested that we should drink a Carlsberg in Geneva Airport at Gate B34: he was returning to Copenhagen and I was returning to London. With the Carlsberg on the table, he asked formally if I would take his job if it was offered to me. I **decided** to agree on the spot but with the caveat that it was only if the Board wanted me unanimously.

When I came back to London after the Geneva trip and told my wife about the conversation with my boss, she was not at all pleased. With then young children being educated in the UK, a nice lifestyle and me being very happy with my job, it was not ideal for the family; however, she agreed that I should accept but only if the offer came from the chairman himself.

However, things immediately became uncertain when the Board **decided** to conduct an internal and external search for the new group CEO through Egon Zehnder. The chairman, Arne Madsen, told me not to worry: 'You will be very pleased that you will be chosen through a formal search process when you get the job. Not if you get the job'. After conducting the internal and external search, the Board did as the chairman had told me it would: I was appointed CEO at the age of 55 with ten years to retirement. I was quite young when I was assigned my first two CEO roles, but quite old when I attained the last one.

When I was appointed Group CEO, I **decided** to use the title Group Chief Executive, which was a choice that stemmed from the negative associations I had with the words 'officer' and 'president'. The CEO title at the time was still a novelty, and the 'officer' element, to my mind, implied somebody who commanded from above and demanded absolute obedience; to me, the title 'president' was associated with banana republics. This was the antithesis of my management style, so I stuck with the title of Group Chief Executive. It is only after retirement that, for the sake of simplicity, I refer to myself as an ex-CEO.

The operational plan for the management succession involved a 12-month transition period, during which the outgoing boss and myself, as Deputy CEO, would act in tandem. As it turned out, the transition period lasted only a few months, and quickly I found myself in pole position much sooner than anticipated.

The negotiations surrounding my package as CEO might be worth mentioning. When I met with my chairman to discuss my package, his first question was about what I expected in compensation. My answer was that I would like to have the same as my predecessor: whilst I suspected that he was very well paid, I did not know the numbers. The chairman said that he could not argue against my logic and I was very happily surprised when I heard the sum involved. He then asked me about the company car: 'Do you want a Jaguar like your predecessor?' I declined as I felt that such a car was too flashy in Denmark where cars are so expensive. My choice was an 8-cylinder Audi A8 4.2 Quattro (another German build) and the chairman approved. When I added that it cost $10,000 more than the Jaguar, he replied that he did not know that you could get cars that were more expensive than Jags. The Audi A8 4.2 Quattro was a navy blue four-door saloon—very different from the white Ford V8 cabriolet and the Jaguar E-type, but technically advanced and fantastic to drive, and so much more discrete than a Jaguar.

My appointment only happened after a very unpleasant internal and external search. A barrage of newspaper articles that drew from inside information and contained much detail about the process and the individuals involved exacerbated the situation.

Two of my three fellow executive Board colleagues decided to resign should I be appointed as they did not want to work for me.

In the event, they both resigned. In retrospect, it is clear that the succession was very badly handled as it contravened three cardinal rules of this process: it was long overdue, it was prolonged and it was public. This created space for all manner of political manoeuvring.

My first period as CEO was marred by fraudulent accounting in our US subsidiary (40% of group sales), which almost led to the bankruptcy of the entire group because we had two syndicated bank loans with 12 banks, who became very nervous. This was an extremely stressful period, and our CFO made the decision to leave. Therefore, I took on the role of acting CFO for a period of six months, which proved to be a very valuable experience for me. My strategy to solve the crisis was to sell the US subsidiary. I believed that our long-troubled US subsidiary caused a 50% discount in the market capitalisation of our group. We sold the business for a price of US$1 to the British service entrepreneur Michael Ashcroft—now known as Lord Ashcroft. The market liked the strategy and, as I had predicted, our market value doubled three months later.

We started a process of developing a new group strategy along the lines of the strategy that I had successfully introduced for Europe and Brazil whilst working in London. One of the first steps was to involve 150 top ISS executives in the process of developing a new strategy. For this, we heavily drew on the inspiration of two professors from Harvard Business School— Jim Heskett and Gary Loveman. We reorganised, we moved headquarters to more appropriate premises, we acquired more than 100 companies and, after five years of my tenure as CEO, the market value of the group had gone up six-fold.

What more could I dream for? This thought never crossed my mind until a certain Easter family holiday at our apartment in Cannes in the south of France. Although I was on holiday, the phone rang constantly, faxes had to be dealt with, and urgent enquiries could not be put on hold. My young daughter quietly let me know that, if I continued to work at this pace, I might not live as long as she would like me to. Her concern made me think and take stock with my wife. The **decision** was then made that I would resign. I felt that this was not only the right **decision** for my family and myself, but it was also the right **decision** for the company. However, I did not want stop working at 60: I wanted a new full-time career with a portfolio of interesting Board positions and assignments.

I handed in my letter to my chairman, Arne Madsen, on a Friday afternoon in July of 1999 when we met before he was going away on his summer holiday. I did not tell him what was in the envelope and he did not open my letter in my presence. When he came back after his holiday, we met again. He said he knew me well enough to realise that I had made a **decision** and that he could not make me change my mind. Nevertheless, he tried with the whole Board present; however, I stuck with my **decision** and argued as to why I thought that they should consider my CFO, Eric Rylberg, as my successor. I knew that it was not my job to appoint a new CEO, but I saw it as my right and duty to propose an internal candidate. After some deliberation, they followed my advice. Eric Rylberg became Deputy CEO and took over from me as soon as his successor as CFO was recruited.

The **decision** to resign five years before the end of my contract was a complete surprise to everybody—the chairman, the Board and my colleagues. But, as said, for myself and my family, it was the right decision at the right time.

During the period spent as CEO, I learnt a number of very valuable lessons, as detailed below:

1. The importance of having a clear long-term strategy that is deeply rooted throughout the organisation.

2. Sustained shareholder value cannot be created if you do not take good care of your key stakeholders, namely employees, customers, shareholders and broader society.

3. Succession is extremely difficult and must be managed cleverly by the Board over the shortest possible period of time so as to avoid internal rivalry.

4. Being Group CEO is a wonderful job if you have a clear strategy, a strong team and a deep knowledge of your business.

5. Beware the arrogance that most certainly will come with success.

MY SECOND CAREER:

When I stepped down as CEO, it did not take me long to build a full 'order book' of interesting positions. Denmark is a very small country and ISS was big there, and for this reason, a CEO of a large group would always be highly visible. The Danes have a pretty apt saying for this: a big fish in a small pond is termed 'world famous in Denmark'.

The steep increase in our shareholder value, our clear strategy and our many acquisitions attracted the attention of the business community. Within a year, I was assigned with the position of Chairman of five Danish companies and sat on five more Boards. Over the years, I substituted some of the Danish Boards by accepting invitations to join the Boards of companies in the UK, Sweden, Germany, Switzerland, the Netherlands and the United Arab Emirates. I also worked for two large private equity firms.

As time progressed, many other interesting opportunities opened up. I became a member of Denmark's first Corporate Governance Committee. I was invited to become an Executive in Residence at IMD in Lausanne, where I spent all my spare time over several years, writing a book about some of my former peers whom I admired. (The book was called *Winning at Service* and sold 10,000 copies on Amazon and 2,000 in Portuguese sold in Brazil.) I lectured on Leadership to MBA Classes at IMD, CBS and at LBS. Other undertakings in the academic world include 10 years on the European Advisory Board of LBS (London Business School) and, since 2007, Adjunct Professor at CBS (Copenhagen Business School).

These opportunities all came about despite the fact that I had only very limited formal management training; in fact, only a one-week President's Course at the American Management Association. My main management and leadership qualifications stem from on-the-job training where I was fortunate to get my first CEO role with total responsibility for strategy, people, customers and P&L at the age of 29.

From the moment I stepped down as CEO, I no longer had to ask any boss or chairman as to which company car I could have. Now was the time to have my dream car. Was it to be the family doctor's 1950 Ford V8 cabriolet? Or perhaps the sleek 1960 E-type Jaguar whose picture adorned the cover of the scrapbook from my student days (which I still have to this day)? No. It had to be a more modern car but a convertible with an 8-cylinder engine. My first choice was a beautiful MGR in racing green, powered by the same V8 Buick engine as found in the Range Rover. Just 2,000 examples of this rare model were produced. It was wonderful to own but, unfortunately, not very practical during my many trips around Europe. What I needed was a modern convertible that would also function as a touring car. The choice was easy: a Mercedes SL 500 with a V8 engine and a steel roof that folds into the boot. This is the car of my dreams— and one that I truly enjoy owning and driving. I intend to keep it always.

During my second career, I learnt many things, as detailed below:

- Each and every stage of a career should bring opportunities to expand one's knowledge and to learn new skills.

- The decade and more I have spent as a member of various Boards has taught me that this body's primary task is to ensure that the company has a clear strategy with the necessary resources to execute and that appropriate emphasis is placed on supervision and follow-up.

- I have also learnt that the owner has the ultimate right to make a decision, and if you disagree with the owner, you have to go. I have made the decision to resign from Boards more than once because I disagreed with the owner.

- I have also learnt that you must carry out very thorough due diligence before you accept Board and advisory positions. Having one 'problem' position in your portfolio is like having one rotten apple in your fruit basket. Not only that, your personal brand will be destroyed forever. With this in mind, I have turned down many invitations.

- When taking on roles as Chairman, I have always spent a lot of time with all stakeholders to understand the role, expectations, strategy, key priorities, authority, etc., and have stated this clearly in an engagement letter to the owners and other key stakeholders.

MY THIRD CAREER:

My second career recently came to an end. Non-executives in Europe must retire when they turn 70 years of age or when they have served on a Board for 9 years in the UK and for 12 years in Europe.

Therefore, at present, I am developing my third career with a portfolio of exciting projects. I am a shareholder and non-executive director in two start-up companies in emerging markets, I write books, I advise companies and individuals, I am a Goodwill Ambassador for Copenhagen, and more will follow. These activities give me more time with my family than I have ever had. This is wonderful. But one thing is certain: I shall never stop being actively involved in interesting projects.

KEY LEARNING IN BUSINESS:

Arguably, the most important single thing that I learnt over the course of almost 50 years in leadership roles is that it is incredible what people can achieve if they are given the opportunity and the right circumstances. I have also learnt that your choice of partner is crucial to your career.

Below I have summarised my career in stages organised by age to give an overview about which jobs I had at which age.

I was quite young when I got my first two CEO jobs, but quite old when I was assigned the Group CEO role. You will notice that I was in my chosen industry and company by my early thirties, and that I had in-depth experience in all key areas of that industry, i.e. sales, operations, logistics, planning, finance and general management.

AGE 24–29: During this time, I was in specialist job as Planning Engineer during my first year with the company, after which I held a number of positions in production, logistics and project management. Very importantly, I had 'people responsibility'. The company was young and fast-growing. I was lucky to move to another country and to be given a variety of middle management positions in functions such as production, logistics, maintenance and project management. Compared with my peers, I was ahead of the curve in career terms.

AGE 29–32: As a General Manager of Kemiform in Brazil, I got my first CEO role—a very small CEO role but at a young age. I had full responsibility over the company, i.e. strategy, people, Profit & Loss, etc. Getting your first CEO job, no matter how small and where it is located, is incredibly important for your career development. If you do a good job in this and the next CEO jobs, you may go far in terms of your career. The move to Kemiform was a big 'double-switch'. I believe that, with the CEO job at Kemiform, I was ahead of my peers in my career.

AGE 32–39: The job as Managing Director and Country Manager of ISS in Brazil was a much bigger CEO role, and I was quite young—even by today's standards. I was on tenterhooks and felt huge responsibility towards the shareholders and employees when I walked through the door on May 2, 1973. The move from Kemiform was a small 'double-switch', i.e. from Functional General Manager in one industry to Managing Director and Country Manager in a very different industry. Again, I believe I was still ahead of my peers in terms of my career.

AGE 39–49: When I left Brazil to take up my new position as Executive Vice President and member of the executive Board of ISS back home in Copenhagen, it was my own choice. I thought I was fully aware of what I had said agreed to. I understood very well the prestige and pay that came with the job. What I had not figured out was that the job as a Country CEO 10,000 kilometres away from the head office is much more independent than the job as EVP at Head Office. Being at the head office meant that my boss was only one floor away, that I could not decide the salary of my secretary, and that my independence had been reduced significantly. My luck was that I spent more than 100 days a year away from my boss and head office when doing my job. I really enjoyed working with the ten country managers who reported to me.

I did not come back from Brazil with the ambition of becoming Group CEO and did not consider myself a candidate. My boss was 12 years older than me, and showed no signs of early retirement. During this period, I had several opportunities to become CEO in other companies; however, on balance, I always decided to stay in the business I knew so well. Only once did somebody else make the decision to stay for me. In career terms, I was no longer ahead of the curve.

AGE 49–55: This period of my life as CEO of Europe, Asia and Brazil was very interesting for me and as rewarding as my job in Brazil. I continued with exactly the same job as I had at headquarters in Copenhagen, although with the big difference that it was away from head office and my boss, and that I got the additional title of Managing Director for ISS Europe Ltd (which included responsibility for Brazil and, later on, Asia). I moved to England and had the best of two worlds. I continued as member of the executive Board with the title EVP, and participated in all group Board meetings. In addition, again, I was an independent operator with the title of Managing Director for Europe, Brazil and Asia (today the tile would be Regional CEO). I moved to London with my wife and three young children. As a family, this **decision** meant so much for all of us. The agreement that I had with the Board was that I should stay in the new job until I retired at the age of 65 years. Both my family and I were extremely excited about this. We set up a small regional head office in London with a team of great people. I could again decide the salary of my secretary, report to a Board and, most importantly, have the freedom to perform that I did not have during my ten years at head office. We refocused the strategy of our part of the business—something I would not have been allowed to whilst at the head office—and the performance of our part of the ISS group improved further. There was so much potential to growing the business for many years to come; however, when I was 54, I suddenly became a candidate for Group CEO. The **decision** to say yes was not simple: my family was very happy in England, and they were not keen on returning to Denmark. However, when I was formally offered the job by the Chairman, I took it. Our three children did not move back to Denmark: I commuted for one year, after which my wife and I moved back to Denmark without our children. It was tough, but luckily it worked out well for all of us. When I got the job as Managing Director and Executive Vice President, this was at the level of my peers. At its conclusion, I had fallen behind.

AGE 55–60: Contrary to my readers, I did not have a career book to inspire me to become CEO of a large global group. However, I achieved the role of CEO in an industry and a company that I knew very well and where my strengths and weaknesses were very well known to everybody.

After having solved a very serious issue with fraudulent accounting in our US business in my first year, I enjoyed the group CEO job a great deal. All the dreams that I did not know that I had were fulfilled over the subsequent four years of my tenure. We introduced a new strategy, reorganised, moved the HQ to less opulent premises, acquired more than 100 companies and increased the value of the company six-fold. Everybody, with the exception of my family, therefore was very surprised when I **decided** to step down as CEO five years before the end of my contract, but I felt that the team and I had achieved so much and that it would be appropriate for me to step down before any potential successors started to position themselves for my job. An important part of my **decision** was also that I now dreamt about a second career for at least another 10 years. I wanted to **re-invent** myself and have a new full-time career with a portfolio of chairmanships, directorships, and advisory and academic roles. It was my judgement that, if I stayed on till I was 65, I would not be able to create such a career. Needless to say, I am well aware that I was behind the curve when I became Group Chief Executive at the age of 55.

AGE 60+: I was very lucky to build up a portfolio of extremely interesting posts very quickly. Six months after resigning, I was Chairman of five companies, Board member of five companies, member of Denmark's first corporate governance committee, executive in residence at IMD, on the European Advisory Board of London Business School, and other roles. I got the roles as result of being a very visible ex-CEO of a very large company in a small country, my network, and a European-wide trend of recruiting foreign nationals as non-Executive Directors to their Boards. My wife and I decided to move back to England when I resigned. As I write this, I have passed the obligatory age of retirement for non-executive directors, meaning I am now in the process of planning and executing a new career. My father passed away at the age of 69, two years after he retired. I shall never retire. I shall always continue to do interesting things.

When I graduated as an Industrial Engineer, formal career planning, the creation of personal brands and having a mentor were not common practices; I guess that some of us must have had some kind of dream or vision that help us shape our careers. I have not had a traditional mentor or a role model during my career. Nevertheless, many people around the world have inspired me. My three bosses have all had enormous influences on the way my career has developed, although I do not regard any of them as a mentor *per se*. A very significant influence on my professional life has been 26 years' participation at World Economic Forum's annual meetings in Davos, where I have been able to meet many of the world's greatest leaders and observe them in action. Several of the big heroes unfortunately destroyed their careers when they became arrogant 'Celebrity CEOs', but that is another story entirely.

Many influences from many sources have shaped my career, and whilst I am loath to name individuals, I make one exception to the rule: my wife, Britta. She has been an excellent mentor in everything I have done in my professional life, somebody who has helped and supported me on my journey 'from local boy to global CEO'. She is my best friend and continues to inspire me.

PART I

THE JOB OF CEO

CHAPTER 1

THE JOB OF CEO

The aim of the book is to inspire you to become a great leader—to be the platform you need to become a successful CEO in a company or industry where your dreams can be fulfilled. We will give you our best advice, but we will also remind you that there is no simple formula to becoming a successful CEO.

A very important piece of advice, however, is this: get a CEO job **as early as you can. No** matter how small it is and where on the planet it is, go for it.

The objective of this chapter is to provide a sense of the job of CEO. This will enable you to understand what you can do to contribute to the success of your company whilst simultaneously developing your career. It should also help you understand whether or not being CEO is the right option for you.

When we talk about CEOs and the role of the CEO, we are not only referring to the CEOs of Forbes 500 companies; what we are dealing with is a very broad spectrum of CEO jobs, as we illustrate in Table 1. There are hundreds of thousands of great CEO jobs out there, ranging from the CEO of your own one-person company to being CEO of a Forbes 500 company.

The term CEO is nowadays used not only for the top job; in a global firm, there will be country, regional and divisional

CEOs. You can also be CEO of your own one-man company. As company or group CEO, you are responsible for 'everything'. If you are a country CEO, you are in charge of your operations in a particular country but not of facets, such as group strategy, shareholders and group resources.

TABLE 1 CEO ROLES COME IN MANY SIZES

CEO	Description/example
S	CEO of your own one-man company CEO of a small local company Country CEO of small operation Regional CEO of small group
M	Country CEO of mid-sized operation CEO of mid-sized company
L	Country CEO of large operation Divisional CEO of large operation
XL	Board member/Divisional CEO of large territory Group CEO of mid-sized or large group COO of very large group
XXL	Group CEO of very large global group

THE ESSENCE OF THE JOB

CEO jobs vary a great deal. Group CEOs are in charge of 'everything' and report to a Board of Directors. If you are the CEO of your own one-man company, you are certainly also in charge of 'everything' and you are your own chairman. The majority of people with CEO titles are typically not in charge of 'everything'. This is very true in, for instance, groups with very complicated matrix structures. Issues of which that they are not in charge include shareholder relations, Board work,

41

the formulation of strategy, and group resource allocation. In order to be a complete CEO you must be in charge of profit and loss, balance sheet, people, customers, execution of strategy and report to a proper Board of Directors.

The role of the CEO is a wonderful role provided you are a great leader, you enjoy it, you are engaged, you are committed and you are available 24/7. This is valid regardless of whether you are the CEO in a huge company or whether you own your own operation. The CEO role is your life, and you do not feel that you are making big sacrifices. Moreover, you have a family life, which commonly blends almost seamlessly with your professional life. Your relatively limited free time is used with great care.

On the other hand, if you are not in control, if you are a micro-manager, if you have a weak team, and if you do not know your business, the role of CEO will most likely be everything but wonderful.

People who become group CEO typically have had three or four smaller CEO positions on their way to the top job. The last job before the top job is often a number two job at company HQ. Being at HQ can be a very difficult period for you: you no longer have the freedom that you enjoyed in your previous country or regional CEO roles, and you may become involved in fierce competition with your colleagues for the top job—and you may be labelled 'a good number two'.

It is very difficult to acquire a Group CEO job—but it is even harder to keep it, which is why the average tenure is so low. About three years.

If you are a CEO, people look up to you. They look for guidance and leadership. All stakeholders (and, quite frequently, the media) put *you* under the microscope. People have an opinion about you.

If you become an important CEO in your environment, you will be invited to all sorts of events. You should not get carried away and become a 'Celebrity CEO': be very selective.

Some sections of the media, politicians, NGOs and the general public often see CEOs as cynical and greedy 'fat cats' who are only driven by their own egos and who cynically operate under the guise of shareholder value. Unfortunately, this viewpoint is sometimes correct. You must avoid this.

The CEO graveyard is littered with ex CEOs who have gone from great leaders to 'Celebrity CEOs' and then the most reviled CEOs. The reason for this is that arrogance often creeps in and they start thinking that the rules no longer apply to them. Being in the top job can be a very dangerous place.

The purpose of business is to make money and to create sustainable wealth for shareholders. However, we hold the view that successful global CEOs do not only manage their companies by the principles of shareholder value; they take a much more holistic approach to their job by applying a stakeholder approach. The rationale for this is that you cannot create value for your shareholders in the long run if you do not at the same time treat your entire stakeholders (customers, employees, suppliers, the environment and broader society) well.

Put simply, great leaders do just three things: (1) they develop strategies; (2) they recruit and develop smart people; and (3) they execute strategies. They work closely together with their teams. All of this is universal and does not depend on culture. However, how they do it may depend on the local culture and other circumstances.

CEOs should only be judged by what they achieve and how they achieve it—not by what they say or the frequency of their media appearances.

Great leaders have the ability to create a shared vision about what kind of company they want to create together with their teams. They are also very good at identifying the values upon which the company should be built and developed. With a shared vision as the guiding star and with sound and well-understood values in place, they take the initiative to develop an exciting long-term strategy through a top-down/bottom-up team planning process in which they play the role of leader and coach.

Group CEOs are in charge of strategy and work closely with their Boards and direct reports (i.e. those who work directly under your supervision) in the team planning process. The direct reports, including regional CEOs, also work with their teams to contribute to strategy development. This concept continues all the way down the hierarchy (top-down) and up again (bottom-up).

Research shows that only 20% of companies stick to their strategy over a long period, and that 80% have changed their strategy in the last 12 months. As mentioned previously, research also shows that the average lifetime of CEOs is approximately three years. However, great leaders do not keep changing their strategies all the time, and they stay in their jobs for lengthy periods. Great leaders understand that strategies must be clear, meaningful to and deeply rooted in the organisation. In companies where the strategy is clear, meaningful and deeply rooted in the organisation, the strategy will not come and go with the CEO.

Great leaders do not sit alone in a dark room or huddled with consultants when they create their vision and develop their strategies: they have a strategic instinct and an ability to drive and inspire the organisation whilst driving the strategy process with their teams.

Developing a great strategy is more art than science: often, you can choose between two or more equally good strategies. The one you decide to go for, with good judgement, will be the best and the one that the organisation should execute relentlessly.

Great leaders are inspiring story tellers with a natural ability to communicate their vision and strategy to employees and all other important stakeholders, including investors. Great leaders give their people a sense of purpose, i.e. why their job and contribution, is important for the success of the business. Incentives are not only tied to the achievement of individual goals but also to producing long-term sustainable goals for the corporation and for individual profit centres.

Therefore, strategy development and implementation is an absolute key task of CEOs.

ASSEMBLE GREAT TEAMS BY RECRUITING AND DEVELOPING SMART PEOPLE

Great leaders understand that it takes great teams with great people to run a business successfully, which is why you often see them recruit people who are smarter than themselves. They do so because they have realised that they do not know everything and that hiring smart people makes them look smart.

Great leaders organise their companies in a way that offers many jobs with a high degree of freedom, transparency and responsibility. This is the best way to discover and develop talent and to enhance performance.

EXECUTION

Great leaders instil a performance culture that encourages everybody to deliver based on a shared vision and clear strategies, and they act as a coach, helping the team with execution.

Relentless execution of the agreed strategy is probably the most difficult of all CEO functions. The distinction between a great leader and a not-so-great leader is more often found in his or her ability to stick to a strategy and to execute the strategy than in developing the strategy.

Many managers are great at telling stories but are very poor at delivering. Great leaders develop a great strategy, stick to it for long periods, assemble great teams, and execute to perfection.

TIME MANAGEMENT

How do successful CEOs spend their time and what do they actually do? There is no simple answer to this question, although there is, however, a huge difference between the way in which a CEO of a small and privately owned business spends his or her time, and how a CEO of a large publically listed global group spends his or her time. Nevertheless, there are certain universal practices that should be routine for CEOs in all parts of the world.

1. Spend more than half their time away from the office coaching and motivating people to execute the strategy and deliver results, learn from customers, etc.

2. When at the office, motivate and coach people to focus on strategy and deliver results.

3. Stay in touch with all stakeholders.

4. Hold regular meetings but leave space in the diary to be available for people and unplanned events.

5. Use one week each year to attend seminars that provide inspiration, education and personal development.

PART II

THE GREAT LEADER

CHAPTER 2

CHARACTERISTICS AND SKILLS OF GREAT LEADERS

We do not believe that great leaders are born, but we do believe that they have an above-average amount of raw leadership DNA that has been identified and developed over time through early and demanding jobs where they have had responsibility for people, customers, and profit and loss in different cultures and business cycles. Such development happens when bosses see the potential and dare to try to unlock their potential by giving them successive challenging jobs. Accordingly, it is about getting roles that really stretch you, as a person, as much as possible in the earliest stages of your career. Some bosses see this as putting high potentials into senior positions early on 'to find out whether they swim or sink'.

Identifying leaders and potential leaders, and developing them is another crucial and difficult leadership task. You can make all sorts of tests and get it wrong; you can interview alone or by committee and get it wrong; you can get it wrong by solely relying on your judgement; if you don't ask tough questions when checking references, you can get it wrong; if you recruit too many team members with the same characteristics and skills as yourself, you also go astray. Even using top search firms is no guarantee of 100% hit rates.

Our collective experience with successes and failures has taught us that great leaders who become successful CEOs have very specific characteristics and skills relevant to CEO jobs. What is more, they have what we would sum-up as 'the right attitude'. Based on these experiences, we have developed three lists outlining the characteristics, skills and experiences that typify great leaders.

THE KEY CHARACTERISTICS OF A GREAT LEADER:

1. Passion for people
2. Strong team player
3. Very high level of emotional intelligence (EQ>IQ)
4. Very high level of energy
5. Balanced personality
6. Sound judgement
7. Curious and eager to learn
8. Integrity and ethical standards
9. Ability to listen
10. Seems lucky

KEY SKILLS OF A GREAT LEADER:

1. Takes initiative and shoulders responsibility
2. Strategic thinker
3. Excellent communicator with people at all levels
4. Reliable: produces results and makes money
5. Interested in all business functions
6. Has intimate knowledge of the business and understands what drives it
7. Understands the big picture and the detail equally well
8. Does not complicate things—keeps it simple
9. Removes roadblocks
10. Makes sound decisions

PEOPLE WHO BECOME GREAT GLOBAL LEADERS HAVE BEEN WILLING, EN ROUTE, TO PUT UP WITH:

1. Working 80 hours a week

2. Often prioritising work over family life

3. Living abroad for several years (with your family), learning new languages and developing knowledge of new cultures

4. Taking responsibility and working under high levels of stress

5. Handling very difficult personnel issues

6. Trusting people

7. Sacrificing pay in your early career if necessary

8. Taking on very different positions to learn all aspects of business

9. Making decisions that are not popular with people around you

10. Not always getting the promotion, pay and titles you had hoped for

CEOs with long-term success have high scores on all three of the parameters in the lists above. In Chapter 4, we will show you how to reflect on these and other topics, and how you should carry out self-assessment tests based on them.

THE LEADERSHIP MATRIX

You can simplify the picture of a great leader as we show in the figure below. If you call development of vision and strategy DIRECTION and combine developing teams and execution under DELIVERY, you get the below matrix with four different leadership profiles:

SETS DIRECTION	The Charismatic Leader	The Great Leader
	The Mediocre Manager	The Effective Manager

EXECUTES WITH TEAM

This is how we characterise the four different leadership profiles:

1. **THE MEDIOCRE MANAGER** is accident-prone and does not achieve much; is low on emotional intelligence and energy.

2. **THE EFFECTIVE MANAGER** takes orders and delivers. He or she is often a great number two person. You need people like this but do not give them the number one job.

3. **THE CHARISMATIC LEADER** is good at telling stories and constantly generating new ideas. However, often, very little comes of the stories and ideas. The organisation becomes confused and loses focus. However, after some time, the more cynical members of management listen politely to their charismatic leader and carry on doing their jobs as they always have done. The naïve members of management jump on the ideas and waste their time. The charismatic leader may appear convincing at first; however, their superficial charm and hidden incompetence will ultimately bring about their downfall.

4. **THE GREAT LEADER** is a great strategic thinker with a passion for people and gets things done. Great leaders make good decisions and do not become arrogant about their success.

Great CEOs have a real ambition to succeed whilst not-so-good CEOs tend to have fear of failure. It is often apparent that many successful CEOs somehow are driven by a dream or a vision, and in some cases an urge to prove to themselves and to others what they are capable of.

CEOs that turn out to be successful are rarely driven by status, power or money, but rather are driven by the challenge, achievements, recognition and the joy of working with great people. Later in the CEO career, with success there is, however, a real risk that some become driven by status, power and money. They become greedy Celebrity CEOs.

In Chapter 4, we will show you how to reflect on your motives for becoming a CEO and how you should carry out self-assessment tests based on these motives.

CHAPTER 3

EDUCATION AND BACKGROUND OF GREAT LEADERS

There are many kinds of education that can lead to the CEO job.

The CEO job is not an academic job but you must have an above-average level of intelligence and a decent education. Your IQ does not need to meet the requirements of the MENSA society (the top 2%) but your EQ (emotional intelligence) must be very strong. Moreover, your GMAT does not have to be above 700.

Typically, you will have 12–13 years of regular school ending with an A-level, Baccalaureate, International Baccalaureate or similar followed by 3–5 years at university, graduating with a bachelors or masters degree. Many of our readers will have topped up their education with an MBA degree.

If you want to pursue a career in business, you have probably had extensive work experiences whilst at college. Furthermore, you must be curious and interested in continuous learning for the rest of your life.

As to your university degree, some people hold the view that what matters is not what you have studied but that you *have* studied and *where* you have studied. A top degree from an Ivy League university will almost certainly secure a promising career in academia, consulting, investment banking etc., but will not necessarily lead to a successful career as a CEO of a global company.

When we look at the educational background of CEOs in large global firms, we have noted some patterns: in the UK, many CEOs have a degree in accounting and have been CFOs before they acquired the CEO position; in Sweden and Germany, many CEOs are engineers; in France, CEOs often have studied political science at the *École des Hautes Études Commerciales* in Paris and spent their early career in the public sector; in the US, many CEOs have degrees in marketing. Such examples illustrate that there is no standard education for CEOs and that the pattern in the countries mentioned is related to the business structure in those countries. Sweden and Germany have large engineering industries. The UK is the financial capital of Europe. In France there are many state-owned or state-controlled companies. The USA is home to the world's largest global brands in many consumer products.

Education and learning at school and university is not the end of your acquisition of knowledge if you want to pursue your career dreams of becoming a global CEO. Learning takes on a whole new dimension once you start working. Learning is a life-long occupation; you will never become too old or too wise to learn. You will learn by working with smart and competent bosses and colleagues, by attending relevant courses, by reading, by being curious, by asking questions (why? and why not?) and by trial and error during work.

When global companies from developed economies used to be called international companies and subsequently multinational companies, many of them employed their own nationals as expatriates in most key positions in every country. The reason for this must have had to do with issues such as control, trust, values, transfer of business knowhow, and often a lack of local talent. Many large multinationals had thousands of expatriates of their own nationality posted around the world. This concept has changed and is continuing to change as a result of on-going globalisation. Global companies have discovered that diversity works very well, that there are many young graduates who are keen to have a global career, and that more and more local talent is available. There is also a cost issue. Posting an expatriate with family to a foreign country is very expensive compared with employing a local person. Furthermore, having expensive expatriates working side-by-side with locals in similar jobs is not always positive for the working climate in a local office. Disparities in pay and conditions can breed resentment.

When considering the way in which global companies from the new world go about their global expansion, it can be seen that they tend to adopt the very same concept with their own expatriates being posted to key positions around the world, including countries in the old world, where talent is available.

Nonetheless, the trend is clear: in the future, what counts is talent and not nationality. When looking at the nationalities of CEOs in very large global companies, we see a trend where more and more CEOs are foreign nationals. The future CEOs and management teams of successful global companies will be true 'Citizens of the World'!

PART III

DO YOU REALLY WANT
TO BECOME A CEO
AND HAVE YOU GOT
WHAT IT TAKES?

CHAPTER 4

REFLECTION, EVALUATION AND SELF-ASSESSMENT TESTS

If your dream is to become a CEO, we suggest that you sit down with somebody who knows you very well, and work through the seven self-assessment tests in this chapter. This person should be a mentor, a senior colleague or a search consultant should you already have a relationship with one. The people who help you with this assessment must be brutally honest, frank and objective—and you must be honest with yourself. Embarking on a CEO career without having what it takes and without being willing to do what it takes can only lead to frustration.

We do not suggest that you put the results on an Excel spreadsheet and score each characteristic on a scale from 0–10 to find an average score within two decimal places; rather, we suggest that you use the traffic light concept to very carefully mark each point in one of three colours, namely green, amber and red.

The result of your assessment tests will fall broadly into three categories. One is where every indication is that you do have what it takes (mainly green). The other is that it is very clear that you do not have it (too many reds). If you are in the middle (mostly green but with quite a few amber lights and perhaps one or two reds) you should try to assess whether you believe that you can improve enough on your weak points to embark on a CEO career track.

Even if you 'fail' in one or more of the self-assessment tests, we recommend that you go through all seven of them. Completing all of the tests and evaluating the results together with your mentor will be valuable for your future career—even should you decide not pursue a CEO track.

WHY DO YOU WANT TO BECOME A CEO?

The first assessment test is about finding out what drives you to consider a career with the ambition to one day becoming a CEO.

TEST 1	First you need to determine your motives:	
TYPE A:	I am primarily driven by the urge to prove my abilities and to work in a team	☐
TYPE B:	I am primarily driven by money and power	☐

If you honestly feel that you are a Type A person, you have passed the test as it is our experience that Type A CEOs generally have more successful careers than Type B potential CEOs.

If you are a typical Type B person, we suggest that you seriously reconsider your motives. If your prime motive is money, power and recognition, you might be able to get a CEO job; however, chances are that you will not become a long-lasting and successful CEO.

ARE YOU WILLING TO DO WHAT IT TAKES TO BECOME A GLOBAL CEO?

The second assessment you should do is to go through our list of 'sacrifices' that you must be willing to make. Ideally, you should not see them as sacrifices because you love what you do and you learn so much. A green light means that you accept whilst a red light means that you do not accept the so-called 'sacrifices'.

The list comes as a package. You cannot pick and choose. In other words, you must ideally find all 11 items exciting and natural to deserve a GREEN light. Too many AMBER lights is a concern. If you have some RED lights, you should definitely not plan for a job as a global CEO. If you want to become a global CEO, your traffic light score should come out like this: predominantly green with perhaps very few amber lights, and definitely no red. If not, the overall result of the assessment-tests may indicate that you have the potential to become a local CEO in a private company or a public organisation.

TEST 2	Am I willing to make 'sacrifices' such as:	GREEN	AMBER	RED
1	Working 80 hours a week	◯	◯	◯
2	Often prioritising work over family life	◯	◯	◯
3	Living abroad for several years (with your family), learning new languages and developing knowledge of new cultures	◯	◯	◯
4	Taking responsibility and work under high levels of stress	◯	◯	◯
5	Handling very difficult personnel issues	◯	◯	◯
6	Trusting people of different cultures	◯	◯	◯
7	Sacrificing pay in your early career if necessary	◯	◯	◯
8	Taking on very different positions to learn all aspects of business	◯	◯	◯
9	Making decisions that are not popular with people around you	◯	◯	◯
10	Not always getting the promotion, pay and titles as quickly as you had hoped for	◯	◯	◯
Total	How many of each colour did you get?			

HAVE YOU GOT THE KEY CHARACTERISTICS OF A GREAT LEADER?

The third test is centred on your characteristics, and once again we remind you that you must be totally honest.

TEST 3	Do I have the key characteristics of a great leader?	GREEN	AMBER	RED
1	Passion for people	◯	◯	◯
2	Strong team player	◯	◯	◯
3	Very high level of emotional intelligence (EQ>IQ)	◯	◯	◯
4	Very high level of energy	◯	◯	◯
5	Balanced personality	◯	◯	◯
6	Sound judgement	◯	◯	◯
7	Curious and eager to learn	◯	◯	◯
8	Integrity and high ethical standards	◯	◯	◯
9	Ability to listen	◯	◯	◯
10	Seems lucky	◯	◯	◯
Total	How many of each colour did you get?			

© 2013 Waldemar Schmidt

Nobody is perfect, so we do not expect anyone to get 10 green lights. A few amber lights are acceptable, but red lights are not good.

DO YOU HAVE THE SKILLS OF A GREAT LEADER?

The fourth self-assessment about your skills that you should carry out is a very deep and honest assessment of yourself on each of the 10 characteristics below:

TEST 4	Do I have the key skills of a great leader?	GREEN	AMBER	RED
1	Takes initiative and shoulders responsibility	◯	◯	◯
2	Strategic thinker	◯	◯	◯
3	Excellent communicator with people at all levels	◯	◯	◯
4	Reliable: produces results and makes money for their business	◯	◯	◯
5	Interested in all business functions	◯	◯	◯
6	Has intimate knowledge of the business and understands what drives it	◯	◯	◯
7	Understands the big picture and detail equally well	◯	◯	◯
8	Do not complicate things—keeps it simple	◯	◯	◯
9	Removes roadblocks	◯	◯	◯
10	Makes sound decisions	◯	◯	◯
Total	How many of each colour did you get?			

© 2013 Waldemar Schmidt

Nobody is perfect, so we do not expect anyone to get 10 green lights. A few amber lights are acceptable, but red lights are not good.

65

DO YOU HAVE THE LEADERSHIP PROFILE OF A GREAT LEADER WITH CEO POTENTIAL?

The fifth assessment we advise you to do is to assess where you think you are on our matrix, and to which point you think that you can move.

If you have not yet had a management job with responsibility, you may find it difficult to score yourself. However, if you try to think about how you have got to where you are in your life now, you will have a sense of whether this has happened by accident or whether it is as a result of your aspirations, skills and characteristics.

TEST 5	Do I have the leadership profile of a great leader?	GREEN	AMBER	RED

HIGH

SETS DIRECTION — DELIVER

The Charismatic Leader
AMBER
~~RED~~

The Great Leader
GREEN

○ ○ ○

The Mediocre Manager
RED
~~NEUTRAL~~

The Effective Manager
AMBER

LOW

EXECUTES Y TEAM

© 2013 Waldemar Schmidt

In this test, we do not expect many to deserve a green light, i.e. the upper right quadrant. But if you are somewhere in the centre of the figure you will deserve an amber light. Needless to say, being at the bottom of the left-hand quadrant will give you a red light and the advice not to go for a career dreaming of becoming a successful global CEO.

WHAT HAVE YOU DONE SO FAR IN YOUR LIFE THAT MAKES YOU LIKELY TO BECOME A GREAT LEADER AND A SUCCESSFUL CEO OF A GLOBAL COMPANY?

This self-assessment is one where you will have to make a judgement on important things that you have done so far in your life.

We suggest that you write the main points as bullet points and then subject each of them to the traffic light scoring system:

TEST 6	What are my achievements in life?	GREEN	AMBER	RED
1	At school, university, sports clubs, etc., was I a leader or a follower?	◯	◯	◯
2	What are my major achievements? Where have I made a difference?	◯	◯	◯
3	Have I had any leadership positions at a young age?	◯	◯	◯
4	Have I taken any major initiatives?	◯	◯	◯
5	Do I always take the traditional route or do I think creatively?	◯	◯	◯
Total	How many of each colour did you get?	◯	◯	◯

© 2013 Waldemar Schmidt

Both green and amber lights are a pass. A red light is not good. If you have not shown any initiative and have not achieved a few great things already, it may not be in your destiny to become a great leader and a successful CEO.

HOW IS MY REPUTATION?

This is also a qualitative test that requires total honesty. You should try to describe how you believe that other people see you as a potential great leader. Please ask your mentor for help to make sure that you get this right.

It is not enough to know what you think about yourself: you must try to find out what your colleagues and bosses think about you. Their opinion will play a key role in the future of your career. We do not suggest that you use traffic lights here; the purpose is simply to provide you with an important outside qualitative view on how you are perceived. This should give you the opportunity to improve where needed.

But how to find out what they really think? You have to ask them! This should be done during your annual assessments with your bosses. You can also ask colleagues to come up with one or two brief points that they think characterise you. Don't forget to ask them to point out weaknesses as well as strengths. You will need three to five honest quotes.

TEST 7	What do my colleagues say about my leadership potential?
1	
2	
3	
4	
5	

The result of this final assessment test should give you two things: first, other people's perceptions of you, which is the only thing that really matters when it comes to career development; and second, the foundation to develop your career and your personal brand.

SELF-ASSESSMENT TESTS RESULTS

You have now been through seven self-assessment tests. The next stage is to write a short and objective essay about the result of your self-assessment tests using the following headings:

1. Why I want to become a CEO

2. 'Sacrifices' I am willing to make to become a CEO

3. Why I believe that I have the *characteristics* of a great leader and the potential to become a CEO

4. Why I believe that I have the *skills* to become a great leader who has the potential to become a CEO

5. My leadership profile

6. My achievements and where I have made a difference

7. What my colleagues say about me

8. Areas where I need to improve

9. Did I pass the test?

10. Decision, action plan, and where do I go from here?

We suggest that you keep your essay in a safe place throughout your career as a precious souvenir of the start of your career.

If you and your mentor(s) are convinced that the results of the seven self-assessment tests indicate that you have what it takes and that you really want to pursue a career that can lead to a CEO job, the next steps will be to start planning your career, creating a personal brand and figuring out how you get on to the CEO career ladder. We will discuss these issues in Part V of *From MBA to CEO*. The self-assessment tests should also give you some guidance as to how big a CEO job you realistically should aim for. We suggest that you are realistic about how far you can go. Focus on getting that first CEO as early as you can—no matter how small it is and where on the planet it is.

If you are just a little doubtful about whether or not a CEO position is right for you, you should consider trying regardless. People with leadership potential typically learn and develop when given the opportunity to show their capabilities. You may have been too modest in your self-assessment. Give it a very serious attempt anyway, starting a career where you have the possibility of getting a small CEO job very early on in your career.

If you have come to the conclusion that a CEO career is definitely not for you, you should start planning a different career and consider creating a personal brand as, 'the effective manager'— an excellent and reliable Number Two man or woman or as a top-notch specialist for which there are many more great job opportunities than there are for CEOs. There are many options.

If you are a woman and have come to the conclusion that a CEO career is right for you but not at this stage of your life because you give priority to raising a family, you should not despair. If you really want to become a CEO *and* raise a family, experience shows that the CFO path to the top can work. Consider building a brand as a rounded CFO with CEO potential.

We have the following advice and comments about this situation:

- Women are often outstanding CFOs and, as such, move to CEO positions if the opportunity arises

- A career break is not necessarily a big problem—even if your male colleagues race ahead

- CFOs can change to another industry much more easily than CEOs

- Whilst raising a family, many good employers will let you work from home on occasion and will understand that you are not ready for a transfer to a new country

- Make an effort to work abroad very early on in your career

- Female CFOs have much higher chances of becoming CEOs than colleagues who have chosen careers in HR, Legal, IT, etc.

- Female CFOs are increasingly in demand for non-executive directorships.

Whatever the outcome of your self-assessment test, you should now move on to Part IV, which covers all key aspects of career planning. This chapter is tailored to people who want to pursue a career towards a CEO role; however, most of the advice will also help people to plan alternative careers.

PART IV

CAREER PLANNING AND
EXECUTION—A LIFELONG TASK

CAREER ADVICE FROM A. DANIEL MEILAND, EX CHAIRMAN AND CEO, EGON ZEHNDER, MBA GRADUATE FROM HARVARD BUSINESS SCHOOL

Making the right decision at the right time is always a challenge, but never more so than when the decision concerns your own career. At every stage of your professional life, in order to succeed, you need a clear view of your goals, an honest appraisal of your personal strengths and weaknesses, and the courage to adopt a complete change of course if the situation demands it.

YOUTH, AGE AND OPPORTUNITIES

Today, career track planning and professional development are often systematically handled by employers. Through regular job rotation, major corporations in particular try to confront their young talents with the greatest possible range of challenges. Mindful of Peter Drucker's thoughts on making best use of career opportunities as they arise, this phase of testing the water and frequent change offers an outstanding opportunity to discover where your strengths lie, identify your preferred work methods, review your values, and get a clear view of your primary objectives. Remember, even highly qualified young executives cannot depend on absolute job security. The corporate restructuring measures of recent years have invariably involved job losses — and there is no sign of that changing. In such situations, no qualifications, however good, can stop you losing your job.

But when the dust has settled, the managers who have 'survived' the turmoil can safely assume that it was not just a question of being one of the lucky few, but that there were also qualitative reasons for their survival.

RESPONDING FLEXIBLY TO CHANGE

Increasingly, the decisive factor is the 'employability' of each individual; their openness and flexibility when faced with change, and their initiative in acquiring skills or experience where these are lacking. The 'survivors' will likely be the career activists who see their careers as projects and themselves as the project managers. The starting point for successful career management is the greatest possible self-knowledge. However, whilst a fundamental review of your strengths and weaknesses leading to a balanced awareness of both sides is essential, it does not mean that these can be changed or moderated at will, or that they necessarily offset one another. When a person emerges from the formative processes of education and early career, he or she will have a firmly moulded personality that, whilst it can be modified or embellished, will retain its core characteristics. As such, it is all the more important to make an honest appraisal of your personality from the outset, and to consider the type of professional environment that would best suit you. Some executives have no taste for the exposure and loneliness of the sole decision-maker and instead prefer to hedge their bets by involving others in the decision process. They feel most at home in an ordered environment, such as they will likely find in a bigger company. Moreover, there are the corporate leaders who thrive best in the clearly structured but unpredictable environment of a smaller company. Perhaps inevitably, many managers kick off their careers in companies that are a poor match for their strengths and weaknesses. Here, resolution and perseverance are called for, as well as the ability to draw one's conclusions and change course when the opportunity arises. Initially, however, every manager should try to attain the maximum in the given setting. An absolute will to give everything your best shot is the decisive criterion in building a successful career. Exceptional performance is the best guarantee that you will be noticed for the right reasons, and that you will find a mentor to support your personal development.

If, however, it becomes clear that you cannot play to your strengths within a specific company, then the time has come to make a change. The ability to make a well-considered change of direction is a key instrument in the career-planning toolbox. It speaks of the kind of energy that can only be an asset for a manager. It is a hallmark of every outstanding executive that they apply their strategic skills not only to corporate policymaking but also in respect of their own personal objectives. Equally, those who are content in their current positions should take care not to lose sight of their own personal goals. If you are going to optimise your career track, you need to be aware at all times of what you want and where you want to be heading. In this way, you will not fail to notice when the time comes for a change of direction. This also implies that a career can embrace several different professions, and indeed such 'patchwork' careers that demand great personal flexibility are becoming more and more common.

EXPERTISE CAREER

Decisions about your career have to be made not only at watershed moments in your biography, but all the time. With this said, we have noticed an increasing pattern of career changes occurring as the first half of a professional lifetime draws to a close. The reason is not so much exhaustion as boredom. Fifteen to twenty years down the career track, the learning curve gradually hit a plateau. The job is less of a challenge and more routine.

The degree of job satisfaction falls off and a long bleak road still lies ahead.

OPTIONS AT THE TURNING POINT

At this point, there are various change options open to an executive. First, they can bid farewell to their past career track and enter virgin territory, perhaps in the context of a move into self-employment. A clear-cut change can lead to an immense increase in the value of the individual's acquired potential, such as when an investment banker joins the management team of a private equity firm or a hedge fund, for example. Second, they can retain their previous management role but, at the same time, develop a complementary, parallel career by accepting a directorship of another company, such as a university teaching post, for example. A third option is to become a 'social entrepreneur' in a not-for-profit role and to scale down the number of hours dedicated to the 'main' job. Top managers often feel a need later in their careers to look beyond personal gain and give something back to society in a pro bono role. However, irrespective of which of these options leads to a second career, the important thing is to begin preparing for it as early as possible, and then put out feelers in the direction of the desired activity. Adopting alternative roles in the second half of life is not only a way of increasing job satisfaction but can also provide some security against setbacks in one's 'original' career.

AVOIDING THE BLACK HOLE

Despite even the best laid plans, any career can be caught in a blind alley. At an advanced age, when the number of alternatives automatically begins to shrink, such situations can be critical. It is not only in the early stages of a career but also towards the end that a clear and realistic view of one's own perspectives is essential. For those who are willing to accept that they have reached the last stop on their career track, without perhaps achieving everything they set out to do originally, there is still no need to begin to shut down systems and for all performance to fade: if you instead focus on all the positive and constructive aspects of your personality and concentrate on exploiting your rich fund of experience, you can derive great satisfaction from managing this final career segment more effectively.

Such a positive approach has an even greater chance of success if accompanied by the opening up of other perhaps non-professional environments. The discovery of new or long-buried interests in private life can help take a more objective view of professional life. When someone finds that, outside their normal profession, they have a valuable and valued contribution to make, they will have a more relaxed and productive approach to work than those who withdraw into themselves. Opening up such sources of meaning and energy is also the best way of managing a post-retirement life. Many managers experience retirement as a black hole; few confront the prospect head-on and many embrace denial. Furthermore, the vast majority turn their attention to the post-retirement phase far too late. Many underestimate the extent to which they have become addicted to a sense of their own importance in both professional and private life. However, upon retirement, managers are also confronted with the banal normality of everyday life. Few are so popular or in demand that they can prolong their active roles by taking up directorships or travel the world as highly paid public speakers. Dealing with the dark phenomenon of surrendering power calls for maturity and creativity. The imponderables of career planning are at their most pronounced in the early professional years and again towards the end; whilst the latter imponderables may be very different, they are no less challenging. The challenge is to know yourself and to demonstrate courage and continuity because, just as it is dangerous to embark on a career without a plan, a will to learn and the firm intention to give of your best, it is no less hazardous to slip passively into unplanned retirement.

Article first published in Egon Zehnder's magazine Focus in 2001

CHAPTER 6

HOW TO LEVERAGE
AN MBA DEGREE

WHEN DOES AN MBA MAKE SENSE? An MBA does not necessarily play a deciding role in the assessment of managers in practice. Relevant, hands-on experience continues to be the most important factor in executive recruitment. An MBA from an elite school, on the other hand, can positively influence hiring decisions.

In assessing managers and presenting qualified candidates to clients, we are commonly faced with the issue of an MBA as an additional qualification (either on a full- or part-time basis). A gap to fill between two jobs and a tougher economic climate are factors recognised frequently as encouraging managers to consider completing an MBA. However, it is important to objectively establish whether or not an additional qualification, such as an MBA, will be useful on an individual basis. Our extensive experience leads us to the following conclusions.

MBAS ARE NOT ALL THE SAME

A clear advantage in a job application and/or the assessment of candidates is a diploma from an elite business school. MBAs are not all the same. The institution that awards the degree is heavily indicative of the quality of the qualification. A diploma from a lesser-known school bears no influence on hiring decisions. An MBA has a clearly positive influence on the decision to hire if two candidates have similar practical experience, but one of the two can offer a highly qualified masters degree. In cases where two candidates have different professional backgrounds, performance records or very diverging profiles, an MBA is of very little significance. If both candidates are still very young and have little professional experience (2–5 years), the MBA-holder tends to come out on top. The older the candidates and the more professional experience they have to offer, the less impact an MBA has on a candidate's success.

When deciding whether or not to do an MBA, the bachelor degree also plays a key role. For candidates with a non-economic background, such as engineers, natural scientists, lawyers and MA holders, for example, an MBA from an elite school is probably more valuable than for those that already have a solid economic background. An MBA is also more relevant if the position in question is a general management post that requires broad strategic thinking, as well as interdisciplinary, interconnected skills. However, in cases where specialist operational expertise is required, an MBA is less pertinent. The international dimension of an MBA assumes greater importance if an international background and an understanding of different cultures are required. For positions primarily based in one country, an international MBA does not give candidates any advantage.

FURTHER EDUCATION AHEAD OF A CAREER CHANGE

It can make sense to get an MBA before making a planned career change as some firms prefer to recruit from schools that specialise in certain sectors and are 'in'. Just as the majority of investment banks look for potential candidates in financially-oriented institutions, IT firms, marketing-oriented consumer goods producers and consulting companies focus on schools that adopt this type of positioning and which offer options relevant to specialising in their programmes.

However, professional and career-based aspects are not the only factors to take into consideration when deciding whether or not to do an MBA. Some experiences can be highly influential on a personal level and enriching in many respects. An MBA can often show managers whether or not they have chosen the right career path to-date as students are faced with realistic case studies from industries with which they are barely familiar during an MBA, as well as different operational set-ups and company situations (start-ups or mature life cycle company). A network of horizon-broadening contacts can also prove valuable in the long-term.

Lastly, the recurring question of whether or not an MBA used to be worth more than it is today is irrelevant. Elite universities are constantly adapting their programmes to reflect the changing needs and conditions of the business world and cannot therefore 'grow old.' On the contrary, the schools often set trends themselves and work closely with the highest profile consulting firms to coordinate the latest management tools and frameworks with their course programmes. Moreover, what an MBA represents in all cases is an awareness of the need for development, namely the motivation and desire to achieve more than others.

An MBA is, however, only a help at the start—a springboard. It is only possible to judge whether or not the investment makes sense in the professional experience that follows. Moreover, there are lots of examples of top CEOs that have made it to the top of their companies without an MBA by virtue of sheer hard work, the ability to assert themselves and steely self-discipline. It is worth considering what one hopes to get out of an MBA in relation to the professional career that should follow it. Secondly, it is also worth checking out the institute in question by verifying its course programme, reputation and positioning. Thirdly, candidates must decide whether or not they can afford the time required to take an MBA (1–2 years) as well as the financial costs (CHF 60,000 to CHF 70,000 per year, plus missed opportunity costs). Finally, an MBA will never be recompensed *per se*; it is the individual that generates added value during the time taken to earn the diploma that will be rewarded.

Article first published in Egon Zehnder's magazine Focus

CHAPTER 7

HOW TO WORK WITH
AN EXECUTIVE SEARCH FIRM

This chapter is designed to convey valuable insights to future CEOs that are not readily available in the market. We will help you understand how executive search firms work and how you can significantly enhance your career prospects by establishing a long-lasting partnership with one of the top five global executive search firms if you dream about becoming a global CEO. These leading companies specialise in serving their clients by recruiting high-calibre executives from about 35-year-old up-and-coming talents.

Aside from the top five global recruiters, there are thousands of large and small employment agencies—both local and regional. These can function admirably for their niche; however, if you want a global career, you should try to partner with one of the top five global search firms.

First of all, it is important that you understand that the top five firms work for their clients and are paid by their clients. They are not in the business of placing candidates. However, they need to know quality candidates they can propose to their clients or from whom they can obtain information about the industries in which they work and about potential candidates for specific assignments.

When a young executive has started to be noticed in his or her industry or function, he or she is likely to start receiving calls from search firms with an opening phrase that often goes like this: 'My name is John, I am a consultant in Search Firm X. Can you talk? ... We have an assignment from one of our clients in the your industry and we are looking for the best candidates in the industry for a position as .... Do you know anybody?' Your first thought could well be that you are getting a job offer; however, this is rarely the case. The best you can envisage is that you might be one of several potential candidates. Nevertheless, the consultant has a much broader agenda: he or she is contacting you believing that you are well placed with knowledge about the industry and that you are in a position to help with names of relevant candidates. This approach shows that search firms do not only rely on candidates already on their files. Search consultants do not only call you; they make as many calls as it takes to identify the pool of candidates they need. If you react positively to the call and are helpful, it is very likely that you will receive more calls from the consultant. This may well give you a valuable opportunity to start forming a very important and life-long relationship with the consultant of the search firm.

If you have not been approached by one of the top-five search firms by the time you are about 35 years old and you have made a name for yourself in your company, industry or in your function, you should be proactive. Conduct some research to establish which search consultants from which firms you should get in touch with. The search firms are organised in practices that cover industries and functions. Ask very discreetly around in your industry to identify the most relevant consultants. When it comes to making contact with your chosen consultant(s), you must be prepared completely. If at all possible, you should try to be introduced to the consultant by someone already well known to them.

In the following section we will detail everything you need to know about building a long-lasting relationship that can pay handsome dividends to both you and the consultant. As with any partnership, it will only work if it is beneficial for both parties.

The benefit to the search firm of working with you is that you will help them do a good job for their clients and that you are likely to become a client yourself when you rise to a senior executive position. The benefit to you is that you will be assisted and guided through your entire executive career, and you might be considered a candidate for executive and non-executive positions when you are ready for this.

A BUILDING RELATIONSHIPS WITH EXECUTIVE SEARCH FIRMS

1. Try to identify the most relevant consultant at the search firm you want to get in touch with (most have consultant profiles on the internet) based on your specific industry, functional expertise or similarity in backgrounds (e.g. business school)

2. Even better, try and find someone who can introduce you

3. Approach the head-hunter in the industry or functional sector where you have proven expertise

4. Take a long-term perspective on the relationship; it is likely to last for many years

5. See it as a two-way street

6. Stay in touch periodically (every 6–12 months)

The executive search profession is relatively young; it has only been in existence for about 60 years and was started in the US. There are now many firms operating in different ways, although there are three main areas of activity. One is leadership search where search firms help companies to find better people to meet their objectives. The second is a family of services known as leadership strategic services where companies are helped to evaluate their teams. The final area is Board consulting, which is all about proper governance, helping to improve the effectiveness of Boards, and helping companies recruit better directors and non-executive directors.

HOW A SEARCH WORKS:

Search firms spend time with their clients to understand what it is they want. Commonly, this is a lengthy process because the client might not grasp entirely what it is they want. The search firm performs quite a lot of research to identify the type of companies where suitable candidates might be found and also to identify the people in those companies who would be suitable candidates. This is a desk research phase, which is followed by an active research phase where contact is made with people and recommendations for potential candidates are sought from industry sources. The search firm will talk to people who may have worked with top-level candidates previously to seek references. Of course they also talk with the candidates themselves to discuss the opportunity and see whether they're interested.

The next step is a short list of candidates. The best of these are interviewed and the very best are presented to the client with a view to taking them on Board.

How do executive search firms work? First of all, they work for clients and not for MBA students. However, executive search firms are always interested in developing relationships with people early in their career because they are going to be the CEOs of the future. Because MBA students and young graduates are future clients, search firms are interested in helping and offering advice. However, there is the need to bear in mind that, as you do not pay them, they do not work for you.

Most consultants will usually work with a number of projects in parallel; usually, this number is between five and ten. If it's more than that, it's quite difficult to be effective; if it's less than that, they are not busy enough.

When you are a candidate in a search, you should expect to get a response—even if the search firm does not expect to present you to the client. However, you shouldn't take that personally if it's a generic response, such as, 'We'll let you know within the next three or four weeks.'

Search firms are very interested in engaging with people who are interested in managing their careers, and they help you gain insights and add value. This is often the start of a relationship that will stretch forward to the time that you become a senior manager and to the time that you become a CEO and a client of the search firm.

Whilst you can usually rely on confidentiality, it is also important to be careful. All of the premium branded firms are very confidential in the way they operate, but that is not always true of some of the smaller players—particularly some of the local players who have often been known basically to try and sell people to the highest bidder. Therefore, it is important that you try to build a relationship with an executive search consultant who you can get on with, somebody who knows your industry sector, somebody who can give you useful advice. Take a long-term perspective on the relationship. It may be that nothing happens for a while, but it's useful because you engage with the individual, you're in the confidential database, they will come back to you, they will talk to you. It should be viewed as a two-way street because search firms can get a lot of value out of developing relationships at MBA level because you have a lot of prospects on the market.

B SOME PITFALLS WE OBSERVE IN JOB SEEKERS

1. Insufficient preparation to understand a client organisation

2. Not asking challenging and insightful questions

3. Being pompous and unpleasant

4. Not being flexible enough in terms of role/responsibility/ compensation package

5. Worrying too much about past lay-offs or a career mistake (though these should be in moderation)

6. Assumption that a 'double-switch' is easy

In terms of some of the pitfalls we observe in jobseekers, firstly, not enough preparation is common, and is something that the client will spot very easily. If you've just walked in to the interview and you don't even know a great deal about the company, the interviewer will spot that quickly and that will count against you significantly.

It is important to ask challenging and insightful questions, probe what the company is about, probe what the brand means, probe what they're doing in China and in Asia.

Don't worry too much about past lay-offs; if you've had periods in your career where you've not been employed, don't get concerned about it. There are many reasons these days why people take breaks in their career, so you do not need to obsess over this.

Never make the assumption that a double switch is easy, i.e. where you switch industry sectors and switch jobs. In any situation like this, you're going to have to deal with a lot of learning curves simultaneously, which increases the amount of risk you'll be under. It requires a great amount of mental ability and a great deal of hard work and not everybody is successful at it. So never assume that a double switch is easy. Try to avoid it and instead make sure that you have a bridge to the next role and then it is more likely to be successful and more likely to progress on your way to becoming a CEO.

C INTERVIEW WITH AN EXECUTIVE SEARCH FIRM

Your CV, if you like, is an elevator speech about you—and it's important that it is very succinct. One record-breaker ran to some 48 pages! CVs on video clips are to be avoided because they're inconvenient and take up too much space on databases. Two succinct pages is absolutely sufficient, and if you cannot describe what you've done in two pages, you should go back and try again.

1. 1–2 pages chronological style. Make it easy to scan in 30 seconds

2. Outline challenges and quantify your achievements

3. Be clear about your responsibilities (people, budget, P&L, geographical scope)

4. Never, ever lie on your CV.

When you interview with an executive research firm, the most important thing to do in any interview is not to talk but to listen. Understand, with the search firm, what the job is about. Moreover, be ready to talk conceptually about your career; why your career moves make sense. Also, it is important to provide examples because, often when interviewing people, we're looking for examples of what they've actually achieved and how they've done it. Given the fact that the time for interview is limited, you need to be ready with such types of example.

Don't be frightened to talk about your successes: it's good to understand what they are and there's no reason to be shy. We should also talk about areas where you've not been successful and what you've done about it because that's very interesting from our point of view and be transparent.

1. Be ready to talk about your whole career—What is the common theme and story?

2. Some questions are best answered with specific examples; have these ready

3. Communicate successes and be open about failures and development areas

4. Be transparent.

D **INTERVIEW WITH A CLIENT**

When you get in front of a client again, it's critically important to listen. The most hollow feedback we get from clients is that the candidate 'was talking all the time' and trying to sell himself too strongly. Never put yourself in that sort of situation.

It's always very important to prepare and to ask very good questions—probing questions. This demonstrates your interest in the opportunity and your interest in the company.

1. Always come prepared and conduct due diligence

2. Remember to listen and to ask good questions. Check back afterwards with your interviewer

3. Don't brag. Strike the right balance between success and learning.

E **TEST AND REFERENCES**

There are a lot of employers who use psychometric testing. These tests can be important ancillary tools but are not the 'be all and the end all'. Search firms also use reference-taking a lot, so when you give the names of references, you should give the names of people who know you well and who can talk authoritatively about what you've actually achieved.

1. Testing is a good complementary tool but should never replace references

2. A good executive search consultant is thorough and obtains references—informal and formal

3. References are about seniority or friendship but should come from people you have worked with.

Working closely with search firms throughout your career can be rewarding immensely for both yourself and the company involved. Ideally, the relationship will evolve as follows:

1. You receive career advice and you help the search firm to understand your industry.

2. You become a candidate, and you may be placed into your dream job one, two or three times during your career.

3. When you move into a senior executive role you may become a client of the search firm.

4. Towards the end of a successful executive career, you will most certainly become a candidate for non-executive Board positions because the search firm knows your strengths and weaknesses so well.

5. The crucial role that a good relationship with a search firm can play at key junctures of your career explains why working with one is so very important.

CHAPTER 8

THE TYPICAL CAREER PATHS OF CEOs

There is not just one avenue that will lead you to a CEO job. Our experience has shown us that your career path is a result of a number of interlinked factors, including the opportunities you are given, your achievements and the choices that you make, as well as in regard to unexpected opportunities that appear suddenly.

We have often seen that people who have had impressive leadership careers were catapulted into leadership positions by someone who believed in them early on. However, there are still some tried and tested career pathways that can enhance your chances of a CEO job as opposed to merely relying on circumstances.

Here are some examples of common career paths to CEO jobs:

MBA: You may start with a large consulting firm where you end up being offered a job with a client company, or you may join a large global company in strategy/business development, after which you gradually move up the ladder in P&L jobs until you eventually are ready for the top job. Other MBAs become entrepreneurs and therefore CEOs in their own companies.

CAREER WITH A GLOBAL BLUE-CHIP COMPANY: Join 'the right company' directly after graduation or after 1–3 years and well before the age of 35 years. In a graduate programme you typically start with one or two different jobs at HQ over a 2-4 year period, where in the second job ideally you have responsibility for people and a budget. From the age of 35–50, you gradually move up from junior management jobs to CEO jobs of increasing size with responsibility for people, budgets, projects, P&L, investments, etc. At around 45–50 years is the time where the really lucky high-performers may be considered for the top job in their group. If you are not chosen, you have various options: you either continue as one of the number two men or women in your company or you try to become Group CEO of a smaller company in your industry. Or if you are prepared to take on a higher risk, you can try a 'double switch', i.e. you change industry and move up the ladder to become CEO in a totally different industry.

THE CFO TRACK: Starts with a degree in accountancy working for one of the top four accounting firms after which you join a client firm (or another firm) where you have one or two financial specialist jobs until you are about 35. At that age you should be with 'the right company' to advance through roles such as treasurer, internal auditor, business controller, CFO of small operation, CFO of medium and larger operations in different countries. When you are about 45–50, you may then move to the CFO position at group level. CFOs often become CEO as a default solution if something unforeseen happens with the sitting CEO and the Board needs a quick solution. An alternative to becoming group CFO could be to become CEO of a large country unit of your group, which will help position you as a credible candidate for the group CEO position if or when it becomes available. In case you see no prospects of your dream job becoming a realistic option for you, you may prefer to leave your company and become a CFO of a larger company in your industry or in another industry. CFO positions are not as tied to one particular industry as are CEO jobs. You may also decide to go for the more risky alternatives, such as a CEO job of in a smaller company in your industry, or to make a double switch and become CEO in a smaller company in a new industry.

MULTI-COMPANY CAREER: There are executives who, for a variety of reasons, end up working for many companies in many different industries. The probability for such people to end their careers as long-term successful CEOs is very low; some do, however, specialise as turn-around CEOs or as CEOs of private equity portfolio companies. Multi-company careers are normally not the results of careful career planning.

ENTREPRENEURS: People mostly become entrepreneurs because they have great ideas and want the freedom of being their own masters and not having bosses. However, entrepreneurs often end up working for somebody, such as banks and investors. If you have the urge to become an entrepreneur, try it out as early as you can. Make a business plan to guide your company and your career and to raise the funds that you need. If you are successful with the execution of your plan, fine; if not, make a career plan and embark on a career as a corporate worker to be in your industry of choice when you are about 35 years of age. The experience as an entrepreneur can be a very valuable asset on your CV if you have learnt something important. There are people who become entrepreneurs by accident, which typically happens if they get involved in an MBO (Management Buy Out) opportunity. To make a judgement about joining an MBO is not only about the fascination of developing a business: you and your family must also make very important decisions about your private finances because you will need to invest. Are you and your partner willing to take a bank loan with collateral in your house? The step from corporate worker is risky but can be very rewarding depending on the 'exit', i.e. the sale of your company. If it goes really well for you, you may have made enough money to become a business angel or to become an entrepreneur. If the exit is not successful, you may have two problems: a financial one and a career-centred one, i.e. who will employ you after a failed MBO or a not very successful MBO? Planning a career as a CEO entrepreneur is a tough task.

FAMILY BUSINESS: We will deal with three different situations here. The first situation is for owners and family members of family businesses who become owner-managers. If your family owns a business and you are expected to become its next CEO after your father or your uncle, we recommend that you work in a couple of very relevant jobs outside your family businesses where you can acquire competencies that are needed for its future success.

The second situation is for people who consider working for family-owned or family-controlled businesses. Many family companies are extremely well run and have strong values. However, many family-owned or family-controlled companies want family members to have key jobs in their firms, meaning that you will have to decide whether or not you want to join a company where it is highly unlikely that you will have a chance to become its CEO.

The third situation is where the owners of a family-owned company decide, for whatever reason, to recruit an external CEO. They are sometimes tempted to recruit a top executive from one of their global competitors. This commonly poses a very serious problem. The top executive from the large global firm is a 'corporate worker', who has advanced through the ranks in a business environment where the company was run as a matrix organisation and multiple support functions were the norm. The transition to a family-owned company with hands-on management most often turn out unsuccessfully for both parties.

THE CONSULTING TRACK: This path to a CEO job is typically one where you join one of the global strategy consulting firms after university or after your MBA degree and stay there for 3–5 years. Having worked with and advised CEOs in your client firms, you then need to start thinking about a career move from advising to executing. Your experience from a highly demanding and professional environment gives you a unique perspective of business and usually a very valuable insight into one or two particular industries and a valuable toolbox. You also develop a network with colleagues and clients that can serve you very well throughout all of your business career. You go through our self-assessment tests and draft a career plan for the path to your dream job. You get yourself a job where your skills can be deployed and tell your new employer what your dream job is. If at all possible, you become part of its fast track programme and become one of their 'high potentials'. The most obvious first role is in a strategy function or in an M&A department.

If you show sufficient interest, the right people skills, etc., it is likely that your next job in the company will be one where you get P&L and people responsibility. Your new job could also be one where you have been part of the team that devised a new business project—which you will be asked to execute. You have now stepped onto the career ladder and will learn from reading this book what you need to do to succeed.

FROM MAIL ROOM TO BOARD ROOM: A generation ago, it was not unusual that you could join a firm as an apprentice or trainee right out of school and move all the way up to CEO—and even to the Chairman position. There are still companies, such as banks and shipping companies, that follow this path, and which typically provide on-going and adequate management training relevant to their industry. Some even sponsor high potentials for their MBA degree. However, even with such well-established programmes in place, these companies often feel that they need to complement their home-grown talent with external talent. This is specifically the case for the very top jobs. Accordingly, it is no longer a safe track for people who dream of a CEO job.

CHAPTER 9

HOW TO CREATE
YOUR PERSONAL BRAND

Personal branding is a process by which we market ourselves to others. A personal brand is not a 'cut and paste' of the profile you write at the top of your CV; a personal brand is about other people's perception of you—and by 'other people' we mean everybody who has a direct or indirect influence on your career.

It is not our objective to write a long and technical chapter about personal branding. If you were to Google, 'How to build my personal brand', you will get all the technical information that you need. In contrast, our objective is to explain why it is important to have a personal brand.

You do not get a top executive position without consciously or unconsciously having built a personal brand. Employers and their recruitment consultants would not have found you if you did not have a very distinct brand which matches their job specifications. Recruitment of top executives is more and more carried out very professionally with the help of executive search firms and based on very detailed specifications of the job, the skills needed, past achievements and personal characteristics.

Your personal brand is your biggest asset. It is the essence of your reputation, and therefore must be developed and nurtured with great care. One big professional mistake or failure can ruin your brand overnight. Over time, a series of great professional achievements will make your brand stand out from the crowd in the space in which you have decided to excel. By standing out, internal and external recruiters will notice you and understand what your next career move should be.

We suggest that, as early as possible, you draft out the personal brand you would like to have in the market—but, importantly, keep it to yourself: don't publish it and don't brag about it. Once you have drafted the personal brand that you would like to have, it is a must that you do not do things that destroy or dilute your brand. Remember, your personal brand is your biggest asset.

As you will discover when you Google, 'How to build my personal brand', there are a number of elements that collectively shape your brand, including:

1. Achievements

2. Industry experience and recognition

3. Functional experiences

4. Skill set

5. Personal characteristics

6. Your values

7. How you dress/personal appearance

8. Hobbies

9. Mobility

10. Family situation.

IN ORDER TO PROTECT YOUR PERSONAL BRAND, THERE ARE SOME PITFALLS OF WHICH YOU MUST BE AWARE:

MEDIA: Most people feel flattered when approached by the media. However, we recommend that you do not overexpose yourself and that you only engage with the media on subjects that are strictly relevant to your business. Once you start talking with the media, it is tempting to go beyond the purely professional. Don't do it.

CELEBRITY STATUS: Avoid falling into this trap. Be careful with 'manager of the year awards', etc.

SOCIAL MEDIA: If you must use this medium, keep it strictly professional and never allow anybody else to post on your behalf. Never post late at night and never post inappropriate comments that could damage your personal brand. Remember that the largest and most popular social media channels often retain copyright of your postings, and they store them permanently. It might be fun now but what will it look like in 20 years' time?

THINGS YOU CAN DO TO INCREASE AWARENESS ABOUT YOUR BRAND:

- **ARTICLES**: Write articles for industry magazines

- **PRESENTATIONS**: Make presentations in industry forums

- **CONFERENCES**: Be selective about which ones you attend

- **NETWORKING**: Industry-specific forums and professional organisations can be a great way of boosting your profile

- **CV**: This should include a very short personal profile that reflects the key features of your professional brand.

In summary, our advice is that you develop a personal brand statement that you keep to yourself and you make sure that everything you do throughout your private and professional life safeguards your most important asset.

CHAPTER 10

HOW TO PLAN AND DEVELOP YOUR CAREER

The purpose of this chapter is to enable you to plan and develop your career. By carefully proceeding through each individual step and figure, you should be able to devise a realistic career plan.

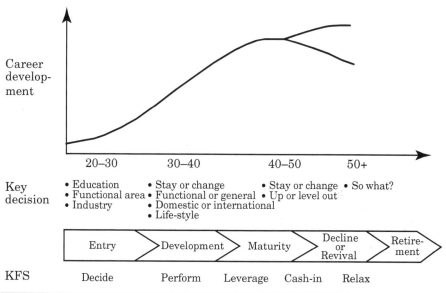

CAREER DEVELOPMENT IS A LIFELONG PROCESS ...

Career develop-ment				
	20–30	30–40	40–50	50+

| Key decision | • Education
• Functional area
• Industry | • Stay or change
• Functional or general
• Domestic or international
• Life-style | • Stay or change
• Up or level out | • So what? |

| Entry | Development | Maturity | Decline or Revival | Retire-ment |

| KFS | Decide | Perform | Leverage | Cash-in | Relax |

© 2011 Egon Zehnder

Career development is a lifelong development. Successful CEOs never stop learning and developing their skills.

A generation ago, career planning was not a common thing. Most successful leaders would say that their career 'just happened' or that they just got lucky. In today's competitive world, however, where bright graduates compete for the best jobs and where great companies compete for the best talent, it makes a lot of sense to make a proper career plan.

Developing a career is a very important management task with three key elements: first, you must have a dream or a vision about what kind of job you would like to have at the peak of your career; second, you must have a plan mapping out how you get there; and third, you must execute this plan.

You must be the CEO of your own destiny. However, this is a task that needs to be executed with a gentle approach. Apply more 'art' than 'science'. No spread sheets, no theoretic models, and no bell curves. Planning a career is not an Excel exercise! You must create an exciting dream ('vision', in CEO language), and you must plan the journey that you want to embark on ('execution', in CEO language).

There will be a strong link between how your career goes and how your family life goes. It is therefore crucial that your partner is very much involved in defining what kind of dream job you are aiming for and what kind of private life this will give you and your family.

You cannot plan your career in every detail. However, your dream must be turned into a road map, which sets out your goal and the direction you are going to take. As a background for drafting your career plan, we suggest that you take a close look at figures 1–10 in this chapter.

As already said and shown in Figure 1, career development is really a lifelong process you never stop. Many great leaders are somewhat off the scale for retirement: they never give up. 'Retirement' *per se* no longer exists; it's more a concept invented by some lazy baby boomers because they wanted to stop work. In actuality, these days you see more and more top executives re-inventing themselves when their executive career ends.

From time to time you should ask yourself: Am I in the right place or should I be somewhere else? Career progression is really all about learning from the time that you start to the time that you do your MBA; from the time that you move into senior functional roles, you move into general management to when you eventually become CEO.

At all stages, the best advice is that you should try and reinvent yourself at regular intervals, give yourself new challenges because that's the only way that you will really progress on the route to becoming a CEO.

Your long-term potential is driven by a number of factors as you will see in Figure 2.

... AND YOU SHOULD AIM FOR A CAREER WHICH FITS YOUR COMPETENCIES, MOTIVATION AND VALUES

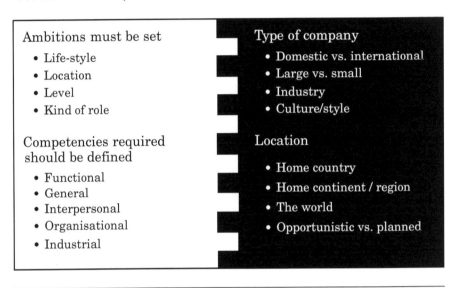

© 2011 Egon Zehnder

The complexity of the above figure illustrates very clearly that there are many factors to be considered when you plan your career. You need to think very carefully about each of the factors: make the right decisions and stick to them.

AMBITIONS, LEADERSHIP COMPETENCIES AND LEARNING ABILITY `FIGURE 3`

Below we deal with all the important aspects of your ambitions, your leadership competencies, and your learning ability.

AMBITION IS CRITICAL: The very fact that you embarked on an MBA and are now reading this book shows that you're pretty ambitious. People have to make quite a lot of sacrifices in order to study to gain an MBA, and ambition is the driving force behind this. You must have ambitions if you want to be successful in business. But you should not only have personal ambitions. To move up the career ladder, your ambitions must include ambitions for your team, for your business unit and very importantly for the company that you work for. When discussing your ambitions with your boss, you should not only ask the question: 'What can the company do for me?' You should also ask the question: 'What can I do for the company?'

LEADERSHIP COMPETENCIES: These are behaviours and capabilities that you develop during the course of your career by being in leadership situations. In order to progress to become a CEO, you need enormous learning ability, which is something that is quite different from ability to learn from books. The critical difference is the ability to take on-board from a whole variety of inputs. We're talking about the ability to ask the right questions; we're talking also about the ability to be very mentally agile, to switch from one subject to the next, to realise when there are certain areas that may no longer be relevant to what you're doing and to move on to new challenges and new ideas.

LEARNING ABILITY: You must have the ability and curiosity to keep learning during your entire career and life. To be a leader means that you must always strive to be ahead.

In order to assess your long-time potential to being a CEO, it is worthwhile to pause for reflection from time to time and ask yourself: Am I learning enough? Am I really interested in becoming a CEO? Becoming a CEO has to be something that you want. It may be that you're grandmother has always told you that you're destined to become a CEO and that your friends think you would make a good CEO, but unless *you* actually want to become a CEO and have the ambition to do so, it's not going to happen.

The figure below shows how your professional platform and brand is created. Over time, you will create a professional platform that is built on four main pillars (function, industry, results and competencies) as can be seen below.

YOUR PROFESSIONAL PLATFORM, PERSONALITY AND LIFE-STYLE CHOICES CREATE YOUR PERSONAL BRAND `FIGURE 4`

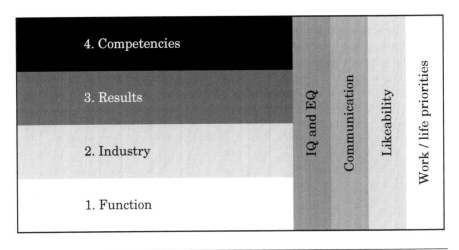

1. Your functional knowledge, which you keep adding to throughout your career. An MBA course is a part of this, as is your initial career development. These need to be maintained and developed continuously.

2. Your industry experience. What sort of industry do you work in? There you should make logical choices that add to your existing competencies.

3. Results are clearly very important because, essentially, that's the way in which you'll be evaluated on your ability to score goals. So it's important that you achieve significant results and typically results ahead of expectations.

4. Competencies, namely critical building blocks, things such as strategic orientation areas, like collaborating and influencing skills, which are very important characteristics and which have important behaviours associated with them, which will take you further forward in your career.

Over time, there is the need to develop a personal brand that is essentially what you are. It is what you have on offer—and that's not only a combination of the four pillars mentioned in Figure 4: It entails a lot of other factors, some of which are relatively 'hard' like IQ and others which are relatively 'soft', i.e. your self-awareness, the way in which you communicate, the extent to which people appreciate you, your likeability. In addition, your work/life priorities are important. For many executives, it is becoming less and less common to make a distinction between work and life; doing so suggests that work is something that is bad and that life is something good, so increasingly we talk about work–life integration, which makes a lot more sense for those of us who actually enjoy what we do.

SIX PIECES OF SOUND ADVICE TO TAKE INTO ACCOUNT WHEN PLANNING YOUR CAREER `FIGURE 5`

1. Make you career dream a journey rather than a destination

2. Think about how you create personal brand and what it should stand for

3. Your dream must be realistic. Do not aim for a Forbes 500 CEO job if you're not certain this is right for you. Aim for one of the hundreds of thousands wonderful CEO jobs that you find in both small, medium and large companies

4. Your dream must not become an obsession. This will be noticed by your colleagues and make corporate life intolerable for you and for your colleagues. Worse still, it could defy the objective.

5. Do not make a career plan where you fail if you do not quite make it all the way. Being a country CEO is often a much more fulfilling job than being an EVP at HQ.

6. Find a mentor to guide you during your early career.

Let our advice sink in and take them into account from start to finish during your entire career.

TEN GOLDEN RULES FOR SUCCESS IN YOUR CAREER `FIGURE 6`

The list below is another source of inspiration throughout your entire career.

---

1. Choose a role that plays to your strengths and life values. Reflect on your competencies and values.

2. Go for blue chip companies early in your career—if you can. They will show you what 'good looks like'.

3. Choose a profession and become accomplished in it. Your professional platform is a key part of your personal brand.

4. Build internal and external networks. A good mentor at the right level is worth gold.

5. Make sure you can give priority to company goals rather than personal ones. Hard work, loyalty and commitment are the most rewarded.

6. Results are what matters. A good career opportunity is a challenge that allows you to show visible results.

7. Work on weak spots and leverage your strengths. Realism about your own competencies counts more than big ego.

8. Go for the challenge, not for the title. A good career move gives you opportunity to prove yourself and show results. Title is less important.

9. Be focused and proactive but not pushy. Take stock at regular intervals and try to be in the 'driver's seat'.

10. Be realistic. It's better to be a top CFO than a weak CEO.

Again, we recommend that you think very carefully about each piece of advice, make the right decisions and stick to them.

It is worth remembering that CEO jobs come in many sizes, and that aiming for the group CEO job in a Forbes 500 company is a very high-risk proposition. There are tens of thousands of great CEO jobs to aim for, so it is important to be realistic in your ambitions. Get that small CEO job as early as possible in your career, and then move up the ladder as you mature and demonstrate that you have what it takes to be a successful CEO.

CEO JOBS COME IN MANY SIZES FIGURE 7

CEO	Description/example
S	CEO of your own one-man company CEO of a small local company Country CEO of small operation Regional CEO of small group
M	Country CEO of mid-sized operation CEO of mid-sized company
L	Country CEO of large operation Divisional CEO of large operation
XL	Board member/Divisional CEO of large territory Group CEO of mid-sized or large group COO of very large group
XXL	Group CEO of very large global group

© 2013 Waldemar Schmidt

Study and understand the structure of the company that you would like to work for, and try to map your way to your dream job as shown in Figure 8. Remember again that a career path is a journey as opposed to a destination. Get the right entry job and start the journey.

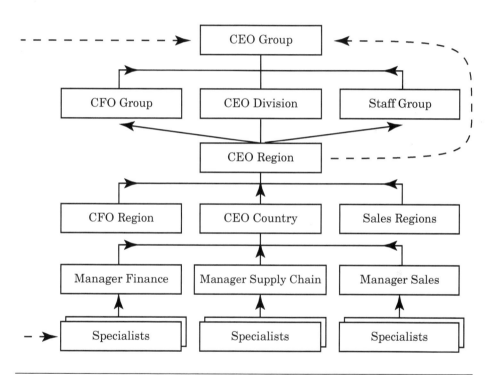

© 2013 Waldemar Schmidt

WHAT COMPANIES SEEK IN HIGH POTENTIAL CANDIDATES

FIGURE 9

The characteristics and skills detailed below are amongst the key areas that companies usually seek. With this knowledge, you should be able to write a compelling CV and a job application that matches what companies seek.

1. Potential, meaning longer term potential to progress throughout your career

2. Strategic thinking capability

3. Ability to drive change

4. Ability to execute and deliver results

5. Ability to win

6. Ability to influence other people.

By also going through our self-assessment tests and your professional experiences, you should be able to write a compelling CV.

At the top of your CV you should consider writing your characteristics and skills as a ultra short 'profile'.

PLAN CAREFULLY FOR YOUR JOB INTERVIEWS THAT SHOULD PUT YOU ON TRACK FOR A CEO CAREER FIGURE 10

The below pre-interview checklist is intended to help you structure your thoughts when you start planning your journey towards your dream job and have interviews with potential employers.

Pre-interview Checklist

Lifestyle:
Location(s)
Level
Kind of role

Competencies required:
Functional
General
Interpersonal
Organisational
Industrial

Type of company:
Domestic or global
Large vs. small
Industry
Culture/style

Location:
Home country
Home continent
The world

Having gone through the ten steps and figures you should now be well prepared for drafting you career plan. We give you some additional guidance in the last part of this chapter with an example:

MY DREAM IS TO:

1. Become the CEO of a medium-sized global group in the X industry.

2. Pursue a second career as non-executive when I retire from my last CEO position

The two points above are provided to illustrate just how precisely your dream should be formulated. Again, we advise you not to be unrealistic. It is much better to over achieve that it is to under achieve.

JOBS I NEED TO HAVE TO REACH MY GOAL:

1. As we have mentioned, career planning is not a science. It's an art. It is much more qualitative than quantitative. And very importantly, remember that it may take up to 20 years of hard work to land a major CEO role.

2. A career plan is something you keep for yourself and don't brag about. It is okay to talk about your kind of dream job. Once you have stepped on to the career ladder, it will be very natural to talk with your bosses about your next job and about your dream job at the annual performance reviews. If you are fortunate enough to become part of your company's fast-track programme for high-potentials, it will also be natural to let your aspirations become known. Your career plan should ideally be in sync with your company's plan for you as a high potential.

3. If you start out young in one of the blue-chip global companies, it would be unwise to go for the top job as an XXXL CEO and tell people about it. There are far too many uncertainties for such a dream to be realistic and the risk of disappointment is huge.

4. When is the right time to draft a career plan? Our experience and research has shown us that most MBAs with CEO aspirations in fact have consciously or unconsciously laid the foundations of a career plan when they decided to go for the MBA degree with the heavy investment that this requires. Few have however made a formal plan.

There are many ways that you can draw up a formal career development plan. For your inspiration, we suggest that you consider a structure as discussed below.

STRUCTURE OF MY CAREER PLAN

1. Join a company that offers me career potential, ideally in a fast track programme for high potentials.

2. Make sure that I am in the right company or industry when I am about 35 years of age.

3. Gain functional experience in finance, sales & marketing and supply chain operations.

4. Work in a minimum of three different countries on two continents.

5. Avoid double and triple switches.

6. Get my first CEO position when I am 35–40 years of age.

7. Get my second CEO position when I am around 40–45 years of age.

8. Get my dream job as Group CEO when I am about 45–50 years of age.

9. Start a new non-executive career when I am 60–65 years old.

We suggest that you use a structure like that outlined above and that you express it in your own words and with as much detail as you deem necessary.

As this is your first draft with the purpose of guiding you in the right direction, it should not be too narrow in its focus. This is in particular relevant in point 1.

Note that we do not include anything about pay. And we only talk about titles when you get your first (small) CEO job. Consistent great performance will over time create your career and secure that you are adequately paid.

If you decide a different career path, such as the CFO route or the consulting route, you will of course have to write your career plan accordingly.

When drafting your career plan you, should also look back to many of the previous chapters for more inspiration.

If your goal is realistic there is no need to change it. However, career plans—as all other plans—have to be monitored and adapted as you go along. And remember that the unexpected happens, which means that you will have to consider opportunities and threats that were not part of your plan. Your judgement is very important in such matters.

Finally, remember that writing a career plan is much more art than science. It is not an excel exercise!

CHAPTER 11

HOW TO GET ONTO
THE CEO CAREER LADDER

You have made your self-assessment and come to the conclusion that you are fit and willing to embark on a career that can lead to a CEO position. You have drafted your personal brand statement, drawn up a compelling CV, formulated a career dream /goal, and you have drafted your first career plan and how you propose to get there. Now, the really critical initial task is to find the right job to start with. A careful reading of the preceding chapters in this book should enable you to do a really good job of getting that crucial first career position. In chapter eight (Typical Career Paths of CEOs) you can find some inspiration regarding the best path to follow for a CEO job. As you can see there are many ways to go about it. If you are clear on the industries you like and which you do not, you should identify the companies where potentially you can have a career that can help you to achieve your goal—and where you think you can make a difference. If you are not quite clear on the industry that you would like to work in, we suggest that you plan to start your career in one or two different industries or companies, where you will gain relevant functional experience in two or more different functions. If you want to pursue the CFO track to a CEO job, you must also try to acquire experience in different functions (accounting, treasury, controlling, etc.) in companies that are recognised as leading-edge in the financial area. We recommend strongly that you also gain experience from a sales and marketing function and in supply-chain functions. We believe that a CEO must have a minimum level of customer experience and operations experience.

Your starting point will be the shortlist of industries and companies you have chosen as relevant to you. In order to prioritise the companies on your list, you should find the answers to a number of questions, including:

1. What business culture do they have?

2. Will they offer me an international career?

3. Do they have a fast track programme? Can I join?

4. Do they have a good track record of employing and developing people like me?

5. How far up the organisation can I get?

6. Do my skills, personality and ambitions fit?

7. Can I become passionate about their products and services?

Once you have done your homework, i.e. produced a comprehensive list of relevant potential employers, you will need to determine how to approach them in the best way. Here are some hints:

1. Large companies tend to be very structured when hiring people like you which means that you must follow their method of graduate recruitment.

2. Smaller companies are sometimes less structured which means that an unsolicited approach could work.

3. Finding companies with bosses with an MBA from your school can sometimes open doors.

4. Networking is important.

Applying for and getting your first job after the MBA is incredibly important, and it requires your complete dedication. The optimum time to leverage your MBA degree is in the first years after graduation. Your MBA School's careers office will organise career activities and will support you in every way it can. But you need to take initiative yourself and put your own resourcefulness to work.

Be the CEO of your own future.

CHAPTER 12

HOW TO CLIMB
THE CEO CAREER LADDER

You have now stepped onto the career ladder as laid out in your career plan and have the prospect of climbing the ladder during the next 20–40 years. Our advice is very simple: there is nothing better for your career than producing excellent results with great teams year after year after year.

In the early part of your career there are a number of things that you must do:

1. Work internationally.

2. Acquire functional experience.

3. Get a job with responsibility for people and P&L as early as you can.

4. Get a CEO job as early as you can. Size and location do not matter.

5. Gain recognition for your achievements, results and team building capability.

This period of your life should be very exciting. There is probably a lot going on in your private life as well: you marry, have children, move to different countries with your family, absorb new cultures, learn new languages, get bigger and bigger jobs, reach the peak of your career and much more besides.

Most successful senior executives would say that the middle period of your life, namely from being around 25–30 years of age to around 50–55, was the most exciting time of their lives. Be prepared for all of this. Enjoy it and get the most out of it.

However, this period of your life will never be all a bed of roses. You will face many difficulties and challenges both in your private life and in your professional life. For example, you may have to consider the availability of appropriate schools and whether your partner can find a job should you a transfer to a particular country. Other conundrums include: Why is it taking so long for my promotion to come through? How do I tackle the issue of underperformance by one of my team members? How do I deal with my boss who I consider incompetent? Should I accept a job offer from a competitor? How do I balance my private life and my professional life? Should I accept an offer to return to HQ? How do I organise my savings and pensions when I keep moving from one country to another? When or where should I get onto the property ladder when I am relocating constantly? My family does not like the country in which we are living but I love my job—what should we do?

There are basically two ways that this middle period can go. The first is that you live the dream and, with determination, ensure that you both reach the goal you set in your career plan and also ensure that your family has had a fulfilling life.

The second way is that everything descends into chaos for yourself and your family because you make poor judgement calls, underperform, fall out with colleagues and bosses, become accident-prone or have family problems.

Tackling problems with a positive attitude will go a long way towards ensuring that your career pans out in the best possible way.

Let us also remind you of the 'Ten Golden Rules for success in your career' that you should observe:

1. Choose a role that plays to your strengths and life values. Reflect on your competencies and values.

2. Go for blue chip companies early in your career—if you can. They will show you what 'good looks like'.

3. Choose a profession and become accomplished in it. Your professional platform is a key part of your personal brand.

4. Build internal and external networks. A good mentor at the right level is worth gold.

5. Make sure you can give priority to company goals rather than personal ones. Hard work, loyalty and commitment are the most rewarded.

6. Results are what matters. A good career opportunity is a challenge that allows you to show visible results.

7. Work on weak spots and leverage your strengths. Realism about your own competencies counts more than big ego.

8. Go for the challenge, not for the title. A good career move gives you opportunity to prove yourself and show results. Title is less important.

9. Be focused and proactive but not pushy. Take stock at regular intervals and try to be in the 'driver's seat'.

10. Be realistic. It's better to be a top CFO than a weak CEO.

Once you have stepped onto the career ladder you need to learn quickly how to manoeuvre successfully in the corporate environment. One important piece of advice is to network but to steer away from gossiping and corporate politics. Be nice to your colleagues and help them when you can.

In order to help you navigate in corporate life during this period we have picked a selection of issues from Chapter 16 'Your A–Z Career Guide', which we think are very relevant for you to look into at this point of your career planning. We suggest that you reflect on the inspiration given below:

ATTITUDE: Great leaders have a positive attitude.

BIGGER JOB IN SMALLER COMPANY: You should be aware that getting a bigger job in a smaller company can be difficult. In a very large company, executives are supported by and dependent upon lots of staff functions. This means that you get specialist advice on all major decisions. You sometimes also have matrix situations where you are not truly independent in your decision making. Move from a job as regional CEO in a large company to a position as CEO in a smaller company can therefore be very difficult. If such a move is a double switch, where you move up one level and change industry, you should be aware that the risk of failure for you and your new employer is considerable. The job as CEO of a small or medium sized company is much more hands-on than a job as regional CEO in a large company. Many employers and owners of small and medium-sized companies dream of employing a top executive from a large global firm without being aware of the risk of failure.

BUILDING TEAMS: Great leaders understand the importance of having great teams with complementary skills around them. They know how to recruit, develop and retain their team members. They are not afraid of giving people challenging jobs.

EXTERNAL OFFERS: All great executives receive approaches from search consultants or directly from other firms with job opportunities during their careers.

MISTAKES: Only people who do nothing avoid making mistakes. When you make mistakes, learn from them and never make the same mistake again. And remember: take the responsibility when you or your team has erred. Also recognise that you do not become a great leader if you constantly fear the failure.

MAKING AN IMPACT: If you wish to become a CEO, your work must make an impact in the company. Throughout your CV, you must have one or more real 'achievements' in each of the jobs that you have had. People who do not make a difference will not become CEOs.

MENTOR: The right mentor (including executive search firms), especially in your early career, can be worth their weight in gold. Get their advice when you need to make critical decisions. Listen to them, but make your own decisions.

NETWORK: Building and maintaining a network of relevant people is very important in your business life as well as in your private life. But remember that a network can only be sustained if it is based on two-way communication. If you receive you also have to give.

NICE: It is better for your career to be nice rather than pushy.

PATIENCE: Great leaders and successful CEOs are normally not very patient when it comes to performance. But during your career there are times when being patient pays off. If you feel that your next promotion is overdue, you may start looking for opportunities elsewhere. But in big organisations unexpected things happen all the time. Some degree of patience may there pay off.

SACRIFICES: Executives who love what they do and who are in control do not feel that they make sacrifices.

SILOS: Many companies are organised by line of business and some by geography. Lines of business are often referred to as silos in management jargon. Moving from one line of business to another in the same company is often very difficult or even impossible. The same goes for geography: if you spend most of your time in one particular region you may get stuck there if you do not make a special effort to move on.

UNEXPECTED EVENTS: Be ready for unexpected events. They will occur. See unexpected events as opportunities. If a CEO role suddenly becomes available in a country in that is not on your list, go for it. If one of your superiors leave suddenly, don't say no to his or her job because you feel that you are not ready for it. If you can swim, you can also swim in deep waters.

CHAPTER 13

BE READY FOR A TOP JOB

When you are 45 years of age or older, you should be in the position where you are ready for the top job as group CEO in your company should it become available. However, it is extremely difficult to foresee just when these jobs become available. It would take a lot of luck to get the timing right. The incumbent may stay until the last day of his contract or may suddenly leave due to poor performance, health issues or a new job somewhere else. Your chances of getting the top job in your group will also depend on competition from internal and external candidates. Aiming for the top job in your company is a very risky strategy. You should therefore prepare Plan B.

Competent Boards have a succession plan in place but often use executive search firms to help them to look at both internal and external candidates for the very top job. Having gotten so far, it is very likely that you are one of the internal candidates. If the departure of the group CEO has been on the cards for a while, it is also very likely that some of the internal candidates in various ways have played political games to position themselves for the top job. The internal competition in these situations is often so fierce that the 'losers' leave the company when one of their peers is appointed as the new CEO.

To be a serious candidate for this job, you will be well-advised to stay out of the political game and be able to demonstrate clearly that you have the following traits:

1. Have a track record from smaller-scale CEO positions of successfully managing a large country, a region or division and having consistently delivered great results and healthy growth

2. Worked in different countries and continents (cultures and languages)

3. Successfully managed businesses through all kinds of business cycles, carried out change programmes and integrated acquired businesses

4. A deep understanding of your business and industry

5. Developed the abilities and career progress of outstanding executives and have a very credible succession plan in place for your part of the group

6. Positively contributed to developing and executing the strategy of your company

In our experience, Boards commonly choose an internal candidate if the company is performing well with no need for a major strategic overhaul. If a major change is deemed necessary, many Boards will appoint an external candidate. This experience should give you an indication of what is likely to happen in your particular case. Boards often choose the CFO for the CEO role because they know him or her better than other internal candidates and see the CFO as a safe pair of hands if no major change is deemed necessary.

Whoever is appointed is chosen because of his or her achievements and talents. If you do get the top job our advice is that you remain your natural self—the person the Board appointed. There is no need to change your personality or modify your modus operandi just because you become group CEO. Remember that your extensive knowledge of the company where you have advanced through the ranks and acquired a strong grasp of key functional areas equips you admirably for the post of Group CEO.

If you get the CEO job, you WILL feel the responsibility. Everybody looks to you for leadership. Your old colleagues, the Board and everybody else recognises that you are the number one with the final say in all important matters.

You must get on with the new job immediately. As discussed in Chapter 1 about the job of the CEO, this is first and foremost about creating long-term shareholder value. We believe that this can only be achieved if you treat all stakeholders with respect.

Remember our simple job description of the CEO role:

1. Develop strategy

2. Recruit and develop smart people

3. Execute the strategy

4. And let us repeat—do *not* lose focus or get carried away if you are successful. Don't become an arrogant Celebrity CEO. Stay with the personality and style that you had when you were chosen for the job.

Your first task will, in likelihood, be to ensure that you have the right team around you. If your peers who did not get the job are not happy they will have to leave, which in turn creates opportunities for other talents.

Your second important job will be to examine the strategy to determine whether adjustments are necessary. Investors, analysts and the media seem to believe that a new CEO means a new strategy after 100 days. In well-managed and well-performing companies, there should not be the need for a total review. In any case, in order to inform all internal and external stakeholders about the company's strategy under your leadership, it would be very wise to make an announcement on the subject as early as possible to remove the uncertainty that the appointment of a new CEO always brings.

Once you have the strategy and your team in place, the job is about relentlessly executing the strategy with your team and overcoming roadblocks and unexpected events. If you are in control and know your business you will soon think that you have the best job in the world and you will enjoy it.

If you did not get the top job in your group, go to Plan B, which is to be considered in the next chapter: Decline or Revival.

CHAPTER 14

DECLINE OR REVIVAL?

The previous chapter was ended by describing the situation where you were an unsuccessful candidate for the Group CEO job in your company.

When you have climbed to a level where you think that it is impossible to continue climbing, or you are otherwise in a situation where you failed to get the top job, you are not a loser. Don't be angry and don't act emotionally. You will regret this. You should instead calmly take stock and consider your options by using your common sense and good judgement.

Amongst the options to consider are the following:

1. Carry on working and delivering happily and loyally, waiting for an unexpected career opportunity may arise in your company or in another interesting company.

2. Your Board may allow you or even encourage you to become non-executive director of one or two companies. This is very interesting and could lead to a CEO job as non-executives occasionally become CEOs in the companies where they serve on the Board.

3. Stay in your job or switch to a specialist position such as head of M&A, IR, HR or seven as CEO of the largest country in your group.

4. Become Group CEO of a smaller group in your industry, but please don't join one of your old fierce direct competitors. This is not fair to your former company where you have enjoyed a successful career. Remember our advice that CEO jobs in smaller companies often require far more hands-on skills than is the norm in large blue-chip companies.

5. Re-invent yourself, perhaps by making a light double switch, i.e. by becoming Group CEO of a company in a similar industry if that role is your absolute priority. However, there are many other alternatives for you to consider: if you are at the right age and financially independent, you may also consider an early non-executive career as discussed in the next Chapter (Retirement or New Career?)

The only thing you should not do at this stage is lose the drive that has shaped your career up until this point. You need to develop Plan B—and execute it. Be the CEO of your own future.

CHAPTER 15

RETIREMENT OR NEW CAREER?

After an enjoyable day on the golf course with friends, many golfers go to 'the 19th hole' (the bar) for a drink and a companionable chat about the day, their golf, and the world. Similarly, after a full day skiing, practitioners of this sport have their *après ski* session in a bar with their friends where they discuss their day's skiing and the world. However, happy endings in the corporate universe are not so simple to attain.

What do executives do when their executive careers have ended after an all-absorbing long life as a global executive? This question is relevant both for executives who did not quite get to the top as they had dreamt about as well as to those who succeeded.

There are several alternatives available of which most fall into one of three categories:

POST-EXECUTIVE CAREER ALTERNATIVES:

1. Become a retiree with no more business activities. You want to be free to do all the things that you were unable to do during your 35–40 years as a busy global executive: improve your golf handicap, spend time on hobbies you have missed, travelling for leisure, tending the garden, spending time with grandchildren, family and friends.

2. Build a portfolio of stimulating Board positions and other part-time jobs to fill one or two days per week. The rest is free for family and hobbies.

3. Embark on a new full-time career for the next ten years with an office either at home or shared with like-minded friends. You could plan for working 40 hours a week and 40 weeks per year, which would be considerably less than you were used to. If you have built a strong personal brand because of your achievements and if you have worked with executive search firms as we recommend, you may be very quickly fully booked with a portfolio of exciting positions. And, as happens for most, you will take on more work than you had planned.

Alternative 1 above is a dream for some; others become bored after 3–6 months and statistics from the life insurance industry indicate that the switch from having a busy career to having no obligations can be very bad for your health.

If you decide to opt for alternatives 2 or 3, we think that the below 10-point checklist will help you to plan a non-executive career:

TEN KEY CONSIDERATIONS WHEN BUILDING A NEW CAREER:

1. Where do you want to live and where should your office be?

2. How should your business card look?

3. Which roles are you most interested in?

4. How to transition from an executive to a non-executive role.

5. How much time will you want to work?

6. How do you remain an independent non-executive?

7. How to avoid conflicts of interest?

8. How to avoid a bad choice?

9. Do you need to administrative support, accountancy and/or legal counselling backup?

10. What are your family's expectations?

If you retire at 60, it is realistic to plan a ten-year non-executive career, after which you will probably want to slow down. If you have enjoyed being a CEO, it is unlikely that you will ever stop doing interesting things.

Finally, make sure that you will be the one to end your business career. If you have never been sacked, you should not let it happen at this stage of your career.

PART V

HOW TO DEAL WITH CRITICAL CAREER AND LEADERSHIP ISSUES

CHAPTER 16

YOUR A–Z CAREER GUIDE

This section of the book is designed as a constant source of inspiration about key leadership and career issues that both young and mature leaders will face during their entire working lives. There are, however no black-and-white solutions. The purpose is to inspire you and help you find your own way in dealing with these critical issues.

ACCIDENT-PRONE: Certain people seem to be accident-prone. Their CVs (resumés) typically reveal a sequence of short stints at many companies without any logical progression—no red thread. When asked why they left their jobs, they usually answer that their company was restructured or that their boss left or the company was acquired. This leaves questions as to why this particular individual was the loser. Do they do a bad job or make a bad judgement call when they joined that company? Regardless, the lesson is clear: don't hire people who seem to be accident-prone.

ACCOUNTANTS: You often meet the argument that accountants will never become great leaders. Wrong! If accountants have the characteristics of great leaders and they decide to manage as general managers and not as accountants, they can well become great leaders.

ACCOUNTABILITY: The more people you can make truly accountable for their business units or functions, the greater will be your odds of delivering your budgets. And delivering your budgets is a key to being promoted.

ACQUISITIONS: Making acquisitions is probably the simplest of all business disciplines. You just pay the price that the seller wants! Moreover, acquisitions are regarded by many executives as one of the most exciting elements of their role. Making acquisitions is also the most difficult of all business disciplines. Just look at the statistics that show that many acquisitions fail to deliver value. Where acquisitions often go wrong in one or more of the following areas: 1) The acquirer does not have acquisition experience and a proper acquisition strategy; 2) There is no robust 'take-over and integration plan' in place; 3) An overambitious CEO simply acquires the wrong company. Importantly, in order to achieve successful growth by acquisitions, you must have a well thought-out acquisition procedure that, *inter alia,* includes the following: 1) A proper acquisition strategy; 2) If yours is a listed company, you must ensure that your investors back your acquisition strategy; 3) Be very disciplined and be willing to say 'no' at times—even if your financial advisors disagree; 4) Involve and commit the managers who are going to be accountable for running the acquired company after the purchase. Do not let your internal M&A team and advisors run the project alone.

ADVISORS: You should never believe that you are a specialist in everything. Therefore the use of advisors and consultants can be crucial in certain very special situations. Ultimately, however, never forget that advisors are advisors: they provide you with good advice. You are an executive and you make decisions and execute with your colleagues.

AGGRESSIVE: A Chinese MBA student at IMD once came to me with a question. His class mates said that he was not aggressive enough to become a CEO. What did I think? Based on my experience, I told him that I do not think that successful leaders are aggressive; rather, they are energetic, persuasive and team players, etc.

AMBITIONS: You must have ambitions if you want to be successful in business, but you should not only have *personal* ambitions. To move up the career ladder, your ambitions must include ambitions for your team, for your business unit and, very importantly, for the company for which you work. When discussing your ambitions with your boss, you should not only ask the question, 'What can the company do for me?' but also 'What can I do for the company?'

ANALYSTS: Many executives disrespectfully refer to financial analysts as '25 year old number crunchers with no clue about their business'. You should never talk disrespectfully about anybody—and definitely not about one of your key stakeholders. We take a different view of analysts. For us, a financial analyst is a stakeholder in the company. We listen to all stakeholders when we formulate company strategy or make very large business decisions. We therefore also listen to financial analysts.

ANALYSES: We know an ex CFO who spent most of his career working for one of the world's 500 largest companies. He told us something very interesting about the two CEOs under whom he had served. The first one got all critical facts right, including a maximum of five key performance indicators (KPIs). He then used his team and his judgement to make decisions. The second one was a maniac with numbers. He always wanted yet another analysis before he made big decisions—and only reluctantly at that. He kept searching for the truth in the figures. Lessons learnt: You must understand and know your business and what drives it intimately; you must know and understand the numbers; you will never find the truth in numbers.

ARROGANCE: Probably the worst enemy of great leadership. If arrogance is an ingrained component of your DNA and you cannot get rid of it, it is highly unlikely that you will have a long career in leading positions. Arrogance does not only stem from your DNA. Successful leaders often become arrogant because of their success. And they do not notice. If arrogance is part of your DNA, you must understand and accept that people see you as arrogant. Thereafter, you must make an effort to change your behaviour and arrange that someone you trust and respect polices your behaviour and gives you honest feedback on your progress in order to ensure you lose the arrogant style. In many cases, your spouse or partner would be the best person to help you with this very delicate task. In order to avoid arrogance creeping in, with success in business you are well-advised to avoid becoming a Celebrity CEO who spends excessive time outside his or her company on Boards, giving speeches at conferences, appearing in the media and ending up as 'Manager of the Year'. Your spouse or partner should help you to remain the genuine person you were when you got the CEO job.

ATTITUDE: Great leaders have a positive attitude.

AVAILABILITY: Great leaders are always available when needed. Some people lock themselves in their office for a week with a 'Do not disturb' sign on the door when they work on a particular project. Some of these people have the ambition to get a leadership position; however, they usually don't make it. However, they are often terrifically valuable specialists as one-man teams. Being available does not mean that you answer mails and calls on your Blackberry or iPhone when you are in meetings or with people. When you are with people you are 100% available to them. However, you should organise your day in such a way that there are enough slots to deal with urgent mails and urgent calls. We know many CEOs who have their email address, mobile number and private phone number printed on their business card, and they tell us that this trust is never abused because they have trained people around them to understand how they work.

BALANCED SCORECARD: This is one of the very few buzz words that you will find in this book. Balanced score cards can be extremely effective if they are kept simple and transparent. Five KPIs—of which three are financial and two are non-financial—are sufficient in focusing on the running of even the largest and most complex businesses. Furthermore, balanced score cards can form the basis for incentive systems.

BEHAVIOUR: Some top leaders start to believe that they are so brilliant and powerful that they are above the law. You have become a CEO because of who you were. Keep learning and keep developing your skills. Just never assume that laws don't apply to you.

BIGGER JOB IN SMALLER COMPANY: You should be aware that getting a bigger job in a smaller company can be difficult. In a very large company, executives are supported by and dependent upon lots of staff functions. This means that you get specialist advice on all major decisions. You sometimes also have matrix situations where you are not truly independent in your decision making. Move from a job as regional CEO in a large company to a position as CEO in a smaller company can therefore be very difficult. If such a move is a double switch, where you move up one level and change industry, you should be aware that the risk of failure for you and your new employer is considerable. The job, as CEO of a small or medium-sized company, is much more hands-on than a job as regional CEO in a large company. Many employers and owners of small and medium sized companies dream of employing a top executive from a large global firm without being aware of the risk of failure.

BLACK OR WHITE: Great leaders do not see business issues as either black or white. It is not as simple as that. Some managers apply the B/W Management concept, but generally without success. If things were this straightforward, leaders would be unnecessary—accountants and computers could be in charge. Another variant that we neither recommend is a concept that was applied by a chemical engineer who became a CEO. He believed that, by breaking business issues down to the smallest particles, he could find the right answers to his problems.

BLAME GAME: Playing the blame game is a no-no if you want to become a great leader. If something goes wrong for you, you don't blame somebody else. You are accountable, you face the problem. Good bosses can take bad news—as long as it is explained properly. Therefore, go to your boss as early as possible to explain what went wrong, why it went wrong, what you have learnt and, very importantly, how and when you are going to fix it. Great leaders take the blame when something goes wrong and attribute successes to their teams.

BOARDS: In your early career, you will probably not have much exposure to the Board and what it does. However, as you get into more senior positions, this will change. You may be involved in preparing papers for the Board, and you may even be asked to make a presentation to the Board. You should know that this happens mainly when the Board wants exposure to talents so you should be extremely well-prepared if you are invited to present something to the Board. Joining the Board is something very special: it is recognition, it feels great, and you become involved in very key decisions surrounding strategy, people issues, etc. One way of learning about the work in Boards is to join the Board of another company as a non-executive. Invitations for this usually come from search firms, which is one more reason why you should find one or two search firms to work with throughout your career. They prefer to propose candidates that

145

they know well. Being a non-executive of a Board will make you a better executive in terms of working with your own Board.

BONUS: Must be simple and transparent to ensure that it serves its purpose, i.e. incentivise managers and staff to achieve extraordinary results. Many bonus programs are far too complicated, short-term and difficult to monitor during the year.

BOTTLENECK: One of the clear signs of a micromanager is when he or she becomes a bottleneck. You must avoid this. Get your priorities right and deal with matters with appropriate urgency. Trust your people and let them get on with their work.

BUDGETS: Budgets must be stretched, but achievable. Delivering or exceeding your budgets year after year is career enhancing.

BUILDING TEAMS: Great leaders understand the importance of having great teams with complementary skills around them. They know how to recruit, develop and retain their team members. They are not afraid of giving people challenging jobs.

BULLDOZING: Bulldozing may do the job. However, it causes a lot of damage, wherefore it is not a technique that is applied by great leaders.

BULLYING: The use of primitive means, such as bullying, will not make you a long-lasting successful CEO. Only weak people who fear losing their jobs put up with bullies. You want smart and independent people around you; therefore, you must stay away from bullying wherever in the world your work takes you! Moreover, if your subordinates are incurable bullies, consider weeding them out: remember that it only takes one bad apple to sour the barrel.

CASH: Companies go broke when they run out of cash. You can pay your bills with cash, but not with EBITDA. Monitor that your business makes real money.

CELEBRATE: Celebrate your successes and you will have more of them.

CELEBRITY CEO: The business world is littered with so called 'Celebrity CEOs'. They are *perceived* to be successful but are often not seen as successful by their shareholders and colleagues. Nobody dares 'touch' them. The symptoms are that their results and achievements are mediocre. However, they speak well, address all sorts of conference, sit on too many Boards, spend too much time with politicians, are media darlings, and have an opinion about everything. They may arrange to have their, have their biographies written, become 'Manager of the Year', go to receptions and cocktail parties, etc. All of this activity means the company's performance suffers. Somebody must stop them when the symptoms start to appear. This can be the chairman, the spouse/partner or a close friend.

CEO: The CEO title is relatively new. Initially, it was only used for Group CEO but is now used widely. The easy way of getting the title is to start your own company—although building your own company is not at all easy. There are companies with 100 country CEOs, 5–10 regional CEOs and one Group CEO. The move from tier four to tier three where you get your first CEO title requires a lot of hard work and outstanding performance. The move from tier three CEO to tier two CEO is much, much harder, but one that you can try to plan for. The top job, Group CEO of a large company is not one that you can plan for. There are far too many unknowns.

CHARISMA: A certain amount of charisma is good and necessary if you want to become a successful CEO. However, if your charisma is huge, and is your main characteristic, it will probably hinder you in pursuing a life as a long-lasting successful CEO. You must also be able to deliver.

COACHING: Be wary of a senior person who wants and needs personal coaching. The vast majority of great leaders have not reached their position by being coached. Use coaching with care and generally only for junior executives for very specific purposes and during a limited period.

COLLEAGUES: Only the group CEO and the Chairman can pick all of their team members. This means everybody else will have to work with many people that they have not themselves selected. This means that you will have to work with colleagues that range from friends to people who never will be your friends. As long as you are colleagues, are competent and do a great job, you must put your personal opinion to one side and work well with everybody.

COMMAND: Some leaders believe that you must give orders to people. 'You do not command people to do a good job. You inspire people to do a good job'. This motto, provided by the founder of Group4, J. Philip Sorensen, is a great philosophy whether you deal with a security guard or one of your nearest colleagues.

COMMUTING: As a global executive, there may well be periods where you have to commute between your home in one country and your office in another; however, you should not do this for very long. Staff in your office may see you as a stranger or not part of the team if you fly away every Friday afternoon and return on Monday morning. Furthermore, it is very likely that your family will also see you as a stranger or weekend guest.

COMPETITORS: Many business people tend to underestimate their competitors. If you have been involved in acquiring competitors you will often have been pleasantly surprised by the strengths of the acquired competitor. Therefore, never underestimate the competition.

COMPLICATED: Many managers have a tendency to complicate matters. One of the characteristics of great leaders is their ability to keep things simple. Spend time and effort on untangling complicated matters before you present them to your team or colleagues. Moreover, teach them to do likewise.

CONFIDENCE: You must have a lot of confidence in your colleagues. However, you should never be over-confident in yourself.

CONFLICTS: Real problems do not go away by themselves and they take focus away from running the business. You must deal with them in a positive manner and not be shy of a potential conflict, however unpleasant at the time.

CONSULTANTS: There are times when it is very wise to use consultants. Nevertheless, it is essential that you remember always that you retain consultants to give you advice. You listen to the advice and you run the business.

CONTROL: Control freaks and micromanagers will never be long-term successful CEOs. You must, of course, have control mechanisms in your business via internal and external audit and business controllers—but not armies of them. The bulk of control should be incorporated within the business model with total transparency through as many as possible profit centres. Having many profit centres can create many CEO jobs, and it makes your great managers and their teams accountable as it shows you who performs and delivers results.

COPYCATS: Leaders do not copy what other people do, but they are often inspired by what other people do. Don't try to copy the way Jack Welsh ran GE in the last millennium; rather, others should be used as a source of inspiration and do things your own way.

CORPORATE GOVERNANCE: Corporate governance started to become the flavour of the month after the Enron scandal in 2001. It is a necessary evil. For many Board members, this became the first tangible tool that they could work with. It should be ensured that the Board work is balanced appropriately between business issues and corporate governance.

CORPORATE WORKER: A corporate worker could be an executive who has spent a long time in a large corporation surrounded by, and supported by loads of specialist staff who need to be consulted about every major business decision. Moving away from such an environment to a smaller firm or, 'worse still', becoming an entrepreneur, often proves almost impossible. Therefore, if you start a career as a corporate worker, you must make an early decision as to the duration of your tenure in that company. Should you stay for a very long time, then you should probably stay put or possibly move to an equally sized company in the same industry. Starting out your career with three to six years as a corporate worker will teach you to value excellence. Achieving concrete results during your tenure will also benefit your future career.

CORRECTIVE ACTIONS: If 'something' (results, projects, etc.) do not go to plan, you must always come up with corrective action (Plan B) when you report the bad news to your boss. Bosses like solutions, not problems. A good boss will, in most instances, accept your Plan B as long as it is credible and as long as it does not happen too often.

COUNTRY CEO: Being country CEO in a global company is often a wonderful job with lots of freedom as long as you perform. A great start of a CEO career can often be to become country CEO at a young age in a small but fast growing business far away from the head office. You will be able to build a young team of great local people and you will be so close to the business and all its functions that you will acquire the skills that you need in finance, sales & marketing, human resources, supply chain, etc. Doing a great job in such a situation will naturally be noticed by your bosses. Small businesses in new markets often attract a lot of attention from HQ. This, in turn, results in a disproportionate amount of visits from HQ, which is a great way of building your brand. The next career moves will often be a series of bigger and bigger country CEO jobs. Subsequently, the inevitable happens often: you become EVP at HQ, which can be very difficult because you become a number two man and lose your freedom.

CRITICISM: You must never criticise a subordinate in public. If they, he or she are/is not up to the job and you have tried to help them to improve, there is only one solution: he or she must move on.

CRS: Corporate social responsibility is about decent behaviour, displayed by the corporation and its people. It is not a department at head office (though these exist). It must be embedded in your corporation's way of doing business.

CULTURES: In a global company, you have different cultures spanning from religion to food, dress code, language, personal behaviour, etc. It goes without saying that cultures must be respected. Having teams comprising different cultures enhances performance. Our experience is that the best way to unify a workforce of many different cultures is to have strong and meaningful values and a clear vision which tells every employee why his or her work is so important for the company to achieve its goals. However, fine words have to be put into practice and the issue of culture must never stand in the way of careers.

CUSTOMERS: Whatever your job, you should always serve customers well, listen to them, and stay close to them.

DECISION-MAKING: As a leader, your job is to make decisions. You often need to decide between two or more proposals that look equally good. You must have that ability to make sound judgements once you have all relevant facts and figures available and you have listened to your team. You will experience that implementation of 'our decision' is usually more successful than 'my decision'.

DELIVER: If you are reliable and deliver on your promises, you will have great career prospects. Ensure that your deadlines, budgets, targets and objectives are all ambitious but realistic so as to make sure you have a chance to deliver.

DIVERSITY: We all have a strange tendency to recruit people similar to ourselves. However, we must remind ourselves that diverse teams produce much better results than teams where all members have the same profile as ourselves.

DOUBLE SWITCH: A 'double switch career move' is when you switch industry and move up one step on the organisational career ladder, i.e. from Country CEO in the pharmaceutical industry to Group CEO in the IT industry. Both you and your new employer must be conscious of the considerable risk that such a move incurs.

DRIVE: You must have drive (meaning a blend of determination and ambition to achieve set goals) to be a great leader, and you must surround yourself with people who also are driven.

EGO: Make sure that you do not have a big ego as big egos do not become great leaders and enjoy long-term success as CEOs.

ENERGY: If you want to be a successful CEO you must have a lot of positive energy and the ability to energise your team. Lazy people don't become great leaders.

ENGINEERS: You often meet the argument that engineers will never become great leaders. Wrong! If engineers have the characteristics of great leaders and they decide to manage as General Managers and not as engineers, they can well become great leaders.

ENTREPRENEURSHIP: Successful CEOs of large global corporations are often corporate workers with a certain amount of entrepreneurship DNA combined with the attributes of great leaders.

EVALUATION: Everybody likes to know how he or she is doing and whether or not his or her boss is happy with their performance. This is particularly the case for ambitious leaders. The best way to measure performance is to have a transparent performance-based business system where performance is measured continuously in the monthly profit & loss, on a project by project basis, etc. Having a performance-based business system has many advantages, one of which is to ensure that all managers always know whether they are doing a good job or a bad job. This avoids big surprises when formal evaluations are made.

EXCUSES: There are no excuses in business. You give explanations followed by what you learnt, what you have done or what you will do about it.

EXECUTIVE SEARCH FIRMS: A vulgar term for executive search firms is head-hunters. The five leading global executive search firms do much more than executive search; they also do Board consulting, leadership strategy services, CEO succession, family business advisory and diversity and inclusion advisory work. In the early stage of your career, you will be mostly interested in the executive search services. However, as you progress, you will become interested in their other services. As with all consultants, the better they know you and the better you know them, the more they can advise and assist you. Therefore, early on in your career you should select a firm to be sparring and working with throughout your entire working life.

EXPATRIATES: There was a time where large multinational corporations had expatriate managers from their home country in all key jobs around the world. We believe this had to do with lack of trust in locals and a shortage of local talents. More and more global companies have learnt that this concept is outdated, de-motivating for local talent, and expensive. Some still use expatriates but for different reasons, such as in the form of a training ground for high-potentials and the transfer of values and know-how.

EXTERNAL OFFERS: All great executives receive approaches from search consultants or directly from other firms with job opportunities during their careers.

EXTERNAL RECRUITMENT: When an external candidate is chosen over an internal candidate, you must always make sure that he or she is seen as much more suitable by the internal candidates who did not get the job. External recruitment is often made when change is on the agenda.

FAILURE AS CEO: CEOs usually fail for one or more of the following reasons: micromanagement, lack of courage and decisiveness to make critical decisions, arrogance, big ego, aggression or inability to withstand pressure. Each of these characteristics makes it impossible to build a strong team and therefore to produce great results.

FAMILY OWNED COMPANIES: In many family-owned or family-controlled companies, it can be a big challenge to make appointments to the top positions. The tendency is often to prefer family members in all key roles—at least for the first few generations. If you consider joining a family-owned company, you should discuss your career potential, i.e. whether there is a glass ceiling somewhere in the hierarchy. If you are the Chairman or CEO of a family-owned company wanting to recruit an external CEO, you should be aware how difficult such a transition is for 'corporate workers'.

FAST TRACK: In the on-going 'battle for talent', more and more large global companies have some kind of fast-track programme for high-potentials. At the same time, more and more young men and women with CEO ambitions make their own career plans and develop personal brands. When planning to hop onto the career ladder, there is the need to explore how you can get in contact with companies whose 'fast-track programmes for high potentials' match your own career plan and the personal brand you want to develop.

FAULT: In business—and, for that matter, in all relations between people—it is not about 'whose fault it is'. It is about taking responsibility. Fault-assigning and finger-pointing are not good terms in business.

FEAR: No organisation performs well in an atmosphere of fear. Fear appears in two different ways. One is where bosses instil a climate of fear. This is obviously not conducive for the working climate and consequently for performance. The other is where leaders are fearful of making decisions—tough or otherwise. Leaders who instil fear in their organisations and leaders who are fearful of making decisions will not become great leaders.

FINISHED: Some people unconsciously work with three versions of the word 'finished' when you asked if they have finished the project for which you are waiting eagerly. You have 'almost finished', 'finished' and 'completely finished'. Being able to tell your boss that your project is 'completely finished' will benefit your career.

FIRE: Don't use the term 'you're fired' except where someone has been dishonest and you want the whole organisation to know that dishonesty is not tolerated. There are so many other terms that you can use when you have to tell a member of your team that he or she will have to move on. Surprisingly, you will often find that underperformers know that they are not in the right place and often are relieved when the pain is over.

FIRST 100 DAYS: There is much talk about 'the first 100 days in your new job'. Each situation is different. Let's take the case of a new CEO. The advice that we will give you if you are a new CEO is: 1) You are being watched by everybody, and everybody expects that you show leadership; 2) Meet as many relevant people and other stakeholders as possible, and be sure to *listen* to them; 3) Don't tell people what you used to do in your previous job; 4) Sit down with your immediate team, discuss your findings, listen to the team and debate your proposed actions and strategy, and gain their commitment to your proposed leadership action. If you are not yet a CEO expected to make and announce decisions, our advice includes: 1) Meet as many people as possible, formally and informally; 2) Ask lots of good questions (Why? and Why not?) and listen; 3) Find out exactly what your new boss, your peers and your team expect from you; 4) Identify those achievements that will help you do a great job and get the next promotion.

FOCUS: Focus is very important but not to the extent that it becomes paranoia. And remember: you can only focus on a few really important matters.

FUN: You should always strive to create a workplace that has an element of fun; this helps performance. A good atmosphere is conducive to good results—your team will benefit if people enjoy going to work.

FUNCTIONAL EXPERTISE: Most executives start their careers with one functional expertise. This could be finance, marketing, engineering or some other competence. If you want to move into general management with the ambition to become a successful CEO, gaining functional expertise in functions that you did not study at university is absolutely essential. A successful CEO has expertise in finance, marketing and supply chain, manufacturing and operations. This enables you to understand all business issues and your colleagues will not waste your time by arguing that 'this does not work with the customer in production of in finance.' You simply become a complete CEO by having functional expertise in all key areas of your business. This argument also supports our view that you should not switch industries late in your career. At the point that you sit down to prepare your career plan you must map out how you will get to spend sufficient time in the two or three key functions where your experience is lacking.

GDP GROWTH: Only companies with 100% market share should be allowed to set growth goals in their budgets that equal GDP growth.

GOALS: Setting the right goals is crucial though difficult. Both near-term and long-term goals have to be ambitious but achievable. If you always reach your goals and always get 100% of your potential bonus, then the goals are not sufficiently ambitious. If you never hit your goals and get no bonus, they are too stretched or your team is underperforming. The 'hockey stick budgets', where near-term goals are undemanding, and long-term goals that are unrealistic all need to be turned down every time you see them. Goals have to be demanding but realistic.

GOLF: Conducting business commonly requires informality within a confidential setting. The golf course can be a perfect solution in the sense that players of vastly different abilities (and both genders) can play a round without anybody raising an eyebrow. Golf is also good for your health! However, it is also time-consuming, which is why few CEOs have low handicaps.

GOSSIP: Becoming party to office gossip (exciting though the titbits might sound) must never be part of your networking efforts; network about what matters for the company and its people. Great leaders steer clear of office gossip and try to counter it when they hear it's going on.

GREAT LEADERS: A great leader is somebody with the capacity to develop clear and feasible strategy, build first-rate teams and execute the strategy. You must become a great leader in order to become a successful CEO.

GREED: Some people are born greedy. Others become greedy with success. Greed is obviously bad for business and must not be tolerated in business.

GREY: You should never think that decision-making is about choosing between black and white. If that were the case, there would be no market for great leaders. Great leaders are the ones that can find the best solutions in the grey area. Appreciate the nuanced picture.

GROWTH: Companies must grow and great companies also grow market share. Growth is good for all stakeholders. Growth creates new jobs, career opportunities, shareholder value and increased tax revenue, all of which benefit society.

HEAD HUNTERS: See executive search firms.

HEAD OFFICE: Spend enough time there to understand the strategy well and to be known for your achievements, but don't stay for overextended periods.

HERO: Great leaders are not heroes: they are leaders of successful teams that collectively on rare occasions stand out as heroes.

HOCKEY STICK BUDGETS: These are budgets where nearby goals are undemanding and distant goals are unrealistic. Never accept hockey stick budgets from your team.

HOPE: Use the word *hope* in small doses in the business world. There is no such thing as MBH (Management by Hope).

HOW TO: Many of us have a tendency to tell our subordinates 'how to do' a given task. This is quite common amongst non-executive directors when in Board meetings. Start asking 'What will you do?' as this encourages initiative and independent thought.

HUMOUR: Always remember that a bit of humour and fun in the workplace increases productivity. Sarcasm has the opposite effect and must be avoided.

I: Certain people always use 'I' and 'me'. Use 'we' and 'us' as a rule and the first person singular only rarely.

INFLUENCE: Great leaders seek influence. Weak leaders seek power.

INITIATIVE: Great leaders take initiatives, relevant initiatives—and see them through to fruition.

INTEGRATION: Great leaders make sure that companies acquired are duly integrated into their companies. They don't leave the acquired company alone; they keep the best people and they don't over-integrate, i.e. destroy the acquired company.

INTERNAL COMPETITION: You cannot and should not try to avoid internal competition in your company. Internal competition is good as long as the individual does not compete at the cost of the team or the company. It is your job as leader to ensure that natural individual rivalry never damages the collective objectives.

INSPIRATION: CEOs draw inspiration from many sources—not by sitting behind their desks. They follow competitors, talk with all stakeholders, read management books, attend a limited number of relevant conferences, and so forth. However, they never go back to the office to copy the last thing that they have heard about. They distil and rework the ideas and use them as inspiration. Remember: leaders are leaders because they don't follow others.

INTEGRITY: If you are the CEO of a global company with tens of thousands of employees in 50 countries it is hard to ensure that a small number of people do not misbehave in spite of your values, controls and business systems. Misbehaviour in a remote place of a global company will spread over the internet instantly. If, or when, this happens, it is important for both external and internal reasons that you act forcefully by explaining what happened and what the consequences were for those who were guilty of the misconduct. You must show that misconduct is not tolerated so as to protect your integrity and prevent a recurrence.

INVESTORS: Investors are the owners of your company. If you are CEO of a listed company, it is important always to remember that you are not the owner. This applies even though, to all intents and purposes, you run the company as if it were your own. The company is owned by institutional investors who have invested in your company because they like what you do. It is an impossible task to keep all investors happy all of the time. Some only stay in for a short time anyhow. However, investors must be treated with respect, i.e. kept informed properly in a transparent way and listened to. Investors and their expectations must be managed as you must manage all of your stakeholders.

IQ: Great leaders do not have to be members of MENSA (a club open to members with an IQ above 132 on the Stanford-Binet scale). However, great leaders are not dumb and are characterised by exceptionally high levels of EQ (Emotional Intelligence). The combination of a good level of IQ and a very high level of EQ is found in the DNA of the vast majority of great leaders.

JOURNEY: We suggest that you think about the goals, objectives and development of your company as a journey rather than a destination. It is not meaningful to the majority of your managers if you state that the company should grow from sales of $100m to sales of $200m over the next five years. It makes much more sense if you state that the company should grow by 15% per annum (for example) for as far into the future as possible. This will energise the organisation and make managers want to contribute to the achievement of the goal.

JUDGEMENT: The ability to make good judgements is key if you want to become a successful CEO. Some have it, others don't. Your ability to make good judgements increases tremendously if you have a competent team, know your industry and your company really well and have your basic facts available. Don't ever think that you can find the truth that you need for your judgement in a spreadsheet, in a model or advice from a consultant.

KNOW YOUR BUSINESS: People with long-term success as global CEOs know their business intimately because they have worked in a number of different functions and different countries/ continents before they reached the top. When the boss knows his or her business, discussions about big decisions become very objective and to the point.

KNOW YOUR NUMBERS: You always have to know your numbers well, but remember that you cannot find the truth in the numbers, no matter how much you analyse them.

KPIS: A total handful of five key performance indicators where three are quantitative and two are qualitative is enough to manage any business. This goes for every level of the organisation. Obviously, there has to be a logical link between the KPIs from level to level within the organisation. Going beyond five KPIs will cause you to lose focus.

LAME DUCK: A lame duck is a person on the way out of the organisation. Make the transition is as brief as possible in order to ensure loss of momentum in the business.

LAWYERS: You often meet the argument that lawyers will never become great leaders. Wrong! If lawyers have the characteristics of great leaders and they decide to manage as General Managers and not as lawyers, they can well become great leaders.

LAZY: Successful CEOs are not lazy—they are full of energy. However, great CEOs often appear relaxed because they are in control and have great teams working for them.

LEADERSHIP COMPETENCIES: These are behaviours and capabilities that you develop during the course of your career by being in leadership situations. In order to progress to become a CEO, you need enormous learning ability; this is something quite different from ability to learn from books. The critical difference is the ability to take on-board from a whole variety of inputs. We're talking about the ability to ask the right questions;

we're talking also about the ability to be very mentally agile, to switch from one subject to the next, to realise when there are certain areas that may no longer be relevant to what you're doing and to move on to new challenges and new ideas.

LEADERSHIP STYLES: There are many styles of leadership and many books are written about the subject. The styles span from 'dictatorial' to 'abdication'. Neither of these extreme styles are found in great leaders. Great leaders have a leadership style characterised by the ability to make great strategic decisions and the ability to assemble and inspire great teams to execute. Great leaders are great because they have a clear strategy and consistently deliver great results by getting the best out of people.

LEADING FROM THE FRONT: We do not think that the term 'leading from the front' characterises the successful global leader. He or she is much more of a coach with the team. He or she is in charge of setting the team, deciding strategy and helping the team win.

LEAVERS: When people, including yourself, leave a company, a distinction is made between good leavers and bad leavers. When you leave, make sure you go as a good leaver. When people leave your organisation, try to avoid having bad leavers, never talk badly about good leavers, and find the right and be brutally honest when asked for references for good leaders as well as bad leaders.

LEGACY: When CEOs get close to the time of retirement, they often want to leave a legacy, such as a new HQ, a mega acquisition (fiercest competitor), etc. Don't do this and don't let other people do it either. The legacies you should leave behind are your achievements and the team that is in place to carry on developing your great company.

LINEAR PROJECTIONS: Great CEOs do not assume that their companies will grow in a linear fashion forever. They do not model the development on a spreadsheet. They set goals that are demanding but achievable.

LONELY JOB: The CEO job should not be a lonely one. Great CEOs are not 'lone wolves'. Nevertheless, there will be some moments where the job of the CEO can feel lonely, as when you are formulating strategies and action that will have dire consequences for people in the organisation.

LOYALTY: You must be loyal to those you work for and with; however, loyalty to your company stands over and above loyalty to individuals should you be in a situation where you must choose between the two.

LUCK: We know that we are not the first to mention this, but the phrase 'the harder you work, the luckier you become' is so true and relevant for your career.

MAKING AN IMPACT: If you wish to become a CEO, your work must make an impact on the company. In your CV, you must have one or more real 'achievements' in each of the jobs that you have had. People who do not make a difference will not become CEOs.

MANAGEMENT JARGON: Use normal language and avoid the use of the latest management buzzwords. It is not good for your career if your people start playing Management BS Bingo when you make presentations or give speeches. The use of plain language simplifies things and eases communication. Jargon complicates.

MANAGER OF THE YEAR: Avoid the nomination if you can! It is our experience that the criteria that award committees use for choosing managers of the year more often than not have very little to do with great leadership and great long-term performance. We have seen many of the 'manager of the year' do very poorly later in their career.

MBO (MANAGEMENT BY OBJECTIVES): We very much agree with management guru Peter Drucker when he said that there should be no other way of management than 'MBO (Management by Objectives)'.

MBO (MANAGEMENT BUYOUT): If you ever become involved in a buyout situation, you must ensure that you choose a side and declare openly which side you have chosen. You cannot work for the buyer and the seller at the same time. If you choose to work with one of the potential buyers and they fail to buy, you only have one choice, i.e. to leave your job.

ME: Always use 'us' instead of 'me'.

MEDIA ATTENTION: When your success as a leader becomes known and you are CEO of a large company, the media will become interested in you. We all like to see our picture in newspapers and magazines—at least in the early years when everything goes well. But when disappointing things happen, most of us could do without it. Therefore, our advice is that you should only appear in the media when it really matters for your company. Don't be one of these CEOs who is willing to comment on anything. Even business journalists speak disparagingly among themselves of 'media tarts'.

MEDIOCRE LEADER: If you're not very good and you just can't cut it, it's time to reassess your position. Moving to a less demanding role would likely benefit both yourself and your company.

MEETINGS: Avoid meetings that are long, have no agenda, involve no decisions being taken, and where no records are made.

MENTOR: The right mentor (including executive search firms), especially in your early career, can be worth their weight in gold. Get their advice when you need to make critical decisions. Listen to them but make your own decisions.

MICROMANAGEMENT: If you are a great leader, you have not become so by being micromanaged by your bosses and not by micromanaging your employees. Micromanagement does not lead to great leadership.

MISTAKES: Only people who do nothing avoid making mistakes. When you make mistakes, learn from them and never make the same mistake again, and remember to take the blame when you or your team has erred.

MOODY: Great leaders are not moody. They maintain a balanced attitude to good and bad news. Moody bosses do not create the kind of work atmosphere that gets the best out of people.

MORAL COMPASS: Whatever your position, ensure you never lose your moral compass.

MOTTO: We think that it makes good sense for companies to have a meaningful and evergreen motto. However, we do not think that CEOs should have their own personal mottos unless they are meaningful and robust, and can last for decades.

NATIONALITY: In a global business, world nationality should not matter but ultimately it still does. Many companies still favour their own nationals when it comes to senior appointments abroad and in HQ. We believe that it has to do with trust and, in the past, a lack of local talent. When joining a company, we make the suggestion that you explore whether there is a glass ceiling somewhere, which down the road will limit your career prospects with the company.

NETWORK: Building and maintaining a network of relevant people is very important in your business life as well as in your private life. But remember that a network can only be sustained if it is based on two-way communication. If you receive, you also have to give.

NEW CEO: When a company announces that there will be change of CEO, it is widely expected that a new CEO means a new strategy for the company. The need for a new strategy should only be there if the company has lost its way or has no strategy. In a well-run company, the strategy may be slightly adjusted. It should be deeply rooted in the organisation and does not need to be changed by a new CEO.

NGO: As the CEO of a global company you are bound to have some NGOs who for a variety of reasons take an interest in your company. Don't consider them a nuisance and don't try to ignore them. NGOs are stakeholders on behalf of society and you need to engage with them accordingly. Be nice.

NICE: It is better for your career to be nice rather than pushy.

NICKNAMES: Great leaders do not use nicknames that are pointed or cruel.

NO: You must have the courage to use the word 'no' in situations where you feel it is appropriate—even if some people do not immediately agree. However, you must explain convincingly your reasons for saying 'no'.

NUMBER TWO GUY: Being a number two guy can be a wonderful job, but if you dream of becoming Group CEO, you must acquire number one positions early on in your career.

NUMBERS: You have to know your numbers and you have to master your numbers, but never let the numbers master you.

You rarely find the truth by going over the numbers again and again.

OBSESSION: Great leaders have passion—not obsession.

OPPORTUNISTIC: There are business situations where you have to be opportunistic. If a business opportunity that is not foreseen in your plans emerges suddenly, and your business instinct tells you that 'this is really interesting, an opportunity we should not miss', then you should use your business acumen and go for it. This should be an exception—not the rule. You may also, out of the blue, be offered a job opportunity in your company or in another fine and relevant company which was not in your career plan. Use your judgement and instinct to make a decision. Don't just ignore the chance. Most people only get one or two 'fantastic' career opportunities in their lives.

OPPOSITION: Business is not like politics where you are either in government or in opposition. In business, everybody is in government.

OPTIMIST: Your chances of being a successful CEO increase greatly if you are an optimist.

ORGANIC GROWTH: Businesses must grow. Growth is good for all stakeholders (investors, employees, suppliers, the tax-man, etc.). A sustainable business must have healthy organic growth, which can be complemented by meaningful acquisitions.

OVERCONFIDENCE: Be confident but not overconfident. Being overconfident can lead to undue risk-taking. It can also lead to very unpleasant behaviour that people around you cannot stand.

PASSION: You mostly hear about passion for people; this is, of course, something that you must have if you want to become a great leader. However, you must also have passion for getting things done, for your company, its values, products, etc. Passion is essential. However, obsession is to be avoided.

PATIENCE: Great leaders and successful CEOs are normally not very patient when it comes to performance. But during your career there are times when being patient pays off. If you feel that your next promotion is overdue, you may start looking for opportunities elsewhere. In big organisations, however, unexpected things happen all the time. Some degree of patience therefore may pay off.

PAY: There will probably be times, especially in your early career, when you are unhappy with your pay. If you are on a career track that has a high probability of leading to your dream job, you should not be tempted to change for a 10% or 20% pay rise. Think about your lifetime income and you will see how little this matters. Salary increases disappoint recipients frequently. However, a constructive dialogue with your boss will go a long way to avoiding repetition. You might learn that your remuneration expectations are too high in this company; at least, however, you should also know how to improve your performance.

PERCEPTION: In a corporate environment, reality matters most but perception should not be ignored.

PERSONAL BRAND: A personal brand should encapsulate what you stand for.

PESSIMIST: Pessimists don't make great leaders.

POPULAR: Great leaders don't seek to be popular. They seek to be respected.

POWER: Great leaders don't seek power. They seek influence.

POWER POINT PRESENTATIONS: Remember that there are times where a one-page memo with your proposal is much more efficient and appreciated than a 10-page Power Point presentation with lots of bullet point and spread sheets. The one-page report will demand much more thought, preparation time and commitment from you.

PROBLEMS: Great leaders do not procrastinate. Delaying dealing with problems often exacerbates the situation.

PROMOTIONS: You will learn that promotions do not always come when you expect them to come. Sometimes, they take longer. If so, be patient. Sometimes, promotions come earlier. If so, be happy.

PROMISES: Always keep your promises.

PUSHY: Be nice, not pushy.

QUALITY: Make sure that the quality of your work is high. Also in the detail.

RECRUITMENT: One of your most important tasks as leader is to recruit people. We all have a tendency to like and recruit people who are as we are. But remember that a strong team has diversity. Not clones of yourself. Be thorough with all aspects of recruitment.

REORGANISATION: In the dynamic global world, we live in there will be times where you have to reorganise. Some people see reorganisations as a threat to their position. People who want to become great leaders often see reorganisations as an opportunity to grow and learn.

RESPECTED: Great leaders are respected. This is not the same as popular.

RESPONSIBILITY: Don't be afraid of taking on responsibility.

RESULTS: The only objective way to judge executives is on their long-term results and how they achieve these results.

REFERENCES: If you are asked for references on someone who has worked for you there are two worthwhile principles to bear in mind: first, ask about the new job so that you can evaluate if it is right for the candidate; and second, be honest. If you give a better reference than the candidate deserves, you will do nobody a favour: the candidate will get a job that he or she cannot do and will lose it quite quickly. The candidate and the new employer are both losers and your own reputation will suffer. Similarly, should you request references for a CEO-candidate whom you are considering hiring, there are three worthwhile principles to consider: first, explain the job in question; second, ask the referee to be honest; and third, ask detailed questions as to the candidate's achievements, strategic skills, leadership skills and personality.

RISK: Business is risky. As a leader, you are constantly faced with having to assess the risks of your decisions. Risks have to be judged and mitigated. However, you cannot run a business without taking risks.

ROLE MODELS: It is very difficult to find a role model who will be of use to you throughout your entire career. It's a bit like education: in nursery school, you had nursery teachers and at university you had professors. Observing the strengths and weaknesses of your bosses and of their bosses can be very educational and a most effective method of life-long learning on the job.

SACRIFICES: Executives who love what they do and who are in control do not feel that they make sacrifices.

SALES & MARKETING PEOPLE: You often meet the argument that sales and marketing people will never become great leaders. Wrong! If sales and marketing people have the characteristics of great leaders and they decide to manage as general managers and not as sales and marketing people executives, they can well become great leaders.

SARCASM: Sarcasm may do well in theatrical plays and stand-up comedies. Don't ever try it in business if your ambition is to become a successful CEO.

SHAREHOLDER VALUE: You cannot create long-term shareholder value if you do not take due care of your employees, customers, the environment and the wider society. There is much academic debate about the relative merits of 'shareholder value' and 'stakeholder value'. We think that this is a rather redundant debate because you can only produce sustained shareholder value if you treat all of your stakeholders (employees, customers, shareholders, the environment and society) with equal decency.

SHORTNESS: 'I made this letter very long because I did not have the leisure to make it shorter,' Blaise Pascal. Learn from this quotation and take the time to make your reports and presentations short and to the point.

SILOS: Many companies are organised by line of business and some by geography. Lines of business are often referred to as silos in management jargon. Moving from one line of business to another in the same company is often very difficult—or sometimes even impossible. The same goes for geography. If you spend most of your time in one particular region you may get stuck there if you do not make a special effort to move on.

SIMPLICITY: Great leaders keep things simple. They do not complicate.

SPECIALIST: The transition from specialist to General Manager is not always easy. You may be a business controller with a high IQ who knows 'everything' about your company and how it should be run; you may impress people around you with the extent of your knowledge; however, if you lack the characteristics and skills of a great leader, it would be better for you to continue your career as a specialist.

SPEED/SENSE OF URGENCY: Great organisations have an atmosphere where speed and a sense of urgency is a constant though not to the extent of hysterical constant stress.

SPOUSE: Spouses often play a very important role behind the scenes in their partner's business success. Of the many advantages of working outside your home country is the fact that your spouse, quite naturally, becomes very involved in your job. You invite colleagues and bosses to your home when they visit your business. Involving your spouse has many advantages, such as sparring, accepting and understanding your long working hours, and allowing your partner to feel more involved in the joint project that is your life together.

STORYTELLING: 'Telling stories' and 'storytelling' are two very different concepts. 'Storytelling' is a great corporate word for the ability to talk with enthusiasm and engagement about your vision for the company, its strategy, goals, values and history. 'Storytelling' is a natural skill possessed by great leaders. On the other hand, 'telling stories' is generally attached to executives who spin a good yarn but who never deliver. It is also a byword for tittle-tattle, gossip or idle talk.

STRATEGY: Successful CEOs embed a strategy within the company that is deeply rooted in the organisation and which creates a sense of purpose for all employees. Strategies should come and go with CEOs.

SUCCESSION: There are two very distinct succession issues that you may come across. The most talked about is that of CEO succession. As a CEO, you have two roles to play in relation to your own succession. One is to have a pool of competent succession candidates in place. Two is to time your departure in such a manner that a bitter fight among the candidates to succeed you is minimised. The timing issue is very difficult because there are always a few more things you would like to do. And this is very dangerous. You see many cases where CEOs want to leave legacies such as large acquisitions. A less talked about succession issue is the one that you will face five or six times in your career, i.e. every time you are promoted. Remember always to have minimum two members of your team who can take your job at about the right time. Also, be prepared for the unexpected promotion. Not all promotions follow the timetable. New opportunities arise when superiors leave the company.

TEAMS: Most of us have a tendency to recruit and gather people around us who are similar to ourselves. This gives us comfort and feels good. However, it is not a good way to assemble high-performance teams. Whether it is a project team or a Board that has to be assembled, diversity works best. Diversity in skills, culture, gender, age and experience that collectively match the task at hand is what you need to perform well. It is unlikely that a Brazilian football team with eleven Peles would have won the world cup.

TECHNOLOGY: Its purpose is to help people become more productive and make better decisions. You are in charge here—don't be its slave.

THANK YOU: Use the term generously but not gratuitously.

TEMPER: Losing your temper in the office is utterly unacceptable. It betrays weakness, lack of self-control, and disrespect for your

174

colleagues. Even if you've done it only once, you should seriously consider whether you have what it takes—and *all* it takes—to become a CEO.

TIME-TO-GO: There are two time-to-go situations for you to think about: one is at the end of your career; the other can be during your career. Both are extremely difficult to deal with as you cannot openly talk with anybody at work about them and you should not let anybody get the sense that you may be considering leaving your job. This is a situation where all your skills and senses will be tested. You depend on your own judgement, ideally supported by your spouse and/or a good friend. The moment your decision to go becomes known in the organisation, you become a lame duck—no matter what people tell you and what you want to believe. When you have decided to go, do so with elegance. Get the timing right and make sure that you have very competent successors in place. Make the transition as brief as possible.

TITLES: Jobs are more important than titles. Some companies are very generous with titles. There are banks with more than 1,000 Vice Presidents. Other companies are less generous. There has also been inflation in titles over the years. The General Manager first became Managing Director, then President and now CEO. A few choose to style themselves 'President & CEO'. Titles are important. We want people to know who we are. Titles are important for the individual and family, in dealings with customers, suppliers, colleagues, etc. However, in the very early part of your career, you should not be obsessed as long as you do not fall behind your peers. Later in your career, when the business card carries the title CEO, it shows that there is only one like you in your company—unlike the bank with 1,000 VPs.

TRANSPARENCY: The opposite of transparency is opaqueness. It is therefore obvious that you, as a great leader, adopt a business approach of transparency.

TRAVELLING: CEOs of large global firms must consider carefully how they most efficiently spend their time—not an easy task. If you are the CEO of a global company with 100 staff at head office and 100,000 employees in 50 countries, you have a serious dilemma. The best decision is often that you spend 40% of your time at your head office and 60% of your time travelling to visit operations abroad, customers and shareholders. And even with such a schedule, it will be difficult to visit operations in all 50 countries with the frequency that both the local country CEO and you would like. Plus, your staff at HQ will tell you that you travel too much. There are ways to mitigate the dilemma, such as through emails, telephone conferences, video calls and management conferences. Nevertheless, you cannot run a global company without a lot of travelling.

TRUST: The opposite of trust is mistrust; therefore, it is obvious that you should always establish a climate of trust in your business. This will get the best out of your team.

UNEXPECTED EVENTS: Be ready for unexpected events—they will occur. See unexpected events as opportunities. If a CEO role suddenly becomes available in a country that is not on your list, go for it. If one of your superiors suddenly leaves, don't say no to his or her job because you feel that you are not ready for it. If you can swim, you can also swim in deep waters.

UNIONS: In many parts of the world, it is very common to dislike unions; however, unions have a role to play and they will not go away. You should therefore consider them as stakeholders and deal with them accordingly through constructive and transparent dialogue.

VALUES: Every company has its formal and informal values, i.e. 'how we do business here and how we don't do business here', 'what are our ethical standards?', etc. Values are created, carried and communicated by people. They are about what you do; not about what you say or write in your manuals, brochures, annual reports and so on. You must identify with the values of your company. When considering moving to a new company, you should make a great effort to understand the values of your new employer by talking to as many of people as you can to ensure that you can identify with these values. As a CEO, you are very much the role-model when it comes to values.

VISION: Successful long-lasting CEOs make sure that their companies have a clear vision which becomes the 'guiding star' for the company's development and which gives each employee a clear understanding as to why his or her job is so important for the company.

VOCABULARY: You will find that use of decent language—not swearing or using dirty words—works much better than the alternative.

WE: Never use 'I' when you talk about your business and its achievements. Always use 'we'.

WHY/WHY NOT?: Use the why/why not concept smartly and you will see that it helps you make better decisions.

WINNING: Always remember that teams should win—not individuals.

WORK–LIFE BALANCE: There are many terrific books about this important subject. The simple version is that it is a matter of priority and mindset. If you really like your job and want to become a CEO, you must set priorities—not necessarily sacrifices. You can do a lot but you cannot do 'everything'.

YES, BOSS!: The 'Yes, Boss' mentality does not exist in companies with great leaders. Great leaders instil a working environment and employ smart people who are expected to express their opinions and not just say 'Yes, Boss!'

ZERO–TEN SCALE: Many managers struggle with determining what is important. A simple method that we have found very helpful has been to ask the question: On a scale from 0–10, how important is this? When posing the question to a CEO who presented an acquisition to his Board he paused for a long time and finally said '5' and added 'I no longer think that we should make this acquisition'.

PART VI

BACKSTAGE INFORMATION

OUR RESEARCH

One question stands out above all others whenever I deliver lectures at business schools. Whether in China or in London or elsewhere, this single question crops up with amazing frequency: 'How do I become a CEO?' This is a pressing question for thousands of MBA students worldwide, and I always seek to answer them as comprehensively as I can either during the session or afterwards on the sidelines. During my time as CEO and subsequently as Board chairman, many young executives have also consulted me on the same subject. This has confirmed my belief that there is huge interest in the topic.

The limitations of the lecture theatre or Boardroom for providing a thorough response are obvious, hence my decision to make my advice available to a much wider audience by teaming up with Egon Zehnder and some of the world's leading business schools to write this book. However, as opposed to simply answering the question that I have heard so many times, I decided to carry out some supplementary research to make sure that all key issues would be addressed. Therefore, we decided to carry out research amongst the students selected from the business schools involved. The purpose of the research project can be broken down as follows:

1. To validate and complement the list of questions that I had assembled over the years.

2. To give the participating students an opportunity to play an active role in the research.

As part of the research, we devised a lecture called 'The job of the CEO...and how you get it', and accordingly presented it at the participating business schools. In the course of these lectures, we shared our findings, had very lively and interactive Q+A sessions and gathered more material for the book.

The research has also helped us design a structure for the book that we believe will make it a life-long companion for many MBAs and others who aspire to become CEOs.

In Part V of the book (How to Deal with Critical Career and Leadership Issues), we address questions that do not naturally fit the structure of the book. Part V also covers our thoughts on questions that were not raised to us, and which fall into the category 'You don't know what you don't know'.

After some initial research work at CBS and LBS, we drew up the following questionnaire and cover note:

Date: _____

To: MBA Students with the ambition of becoming CEOs

From: Waldemar Schmidt

Ref: Invitation to participate in book project: From MBA to CEO
        (career planning from A–Z)

Dear busy MBA student,

I am a very experienced global CEO & Chairman, who has
teamed up with the leading global search firm Egon Zehnder
and some of the world's leading business schools to write a book
with the working title *From MBA to CEO*.

The team has, over the years, interacted with many MBA
students and graduates about how to plan and develop a career
that can lead to a CEO role. Many questions have been asked
and answered. We now want to make our experience available
to MBA students around the world in the form of a book. Our
search has shown us that there are no books on this subject.
Our book will be tailor-made to the specific needs of our future
readers. We are very ambitious as we aim at writing a book
that will become recognised as *the* global reference book on
the subject. In order to make sure that we cover all issues of
relevance, we will carry out a research project amongst MBA
students.

All royalty income from the sale of the book will go towards
a scholarship that we will set up for future students at
participating business schools.

You have been selected to join our *From MBA to CEO* book community by participating in our research project with the opportunity to have your name mentioned in the book if you wish.

The book will have the following building blocks: 1. The job of the CEO, 2. Career planning and life-long career development, and 3. Leadership challenges.

All you need to do is to carefully fill in the attached qualitative research questionnaire, and return it to mba2ceobook@gmail.com within ten days of receiving this invitation.

Egon Zehnder and Waldemar Schmidt will be visiting the participating business schools to give a joint lecture ('The Job of the CEO... and how you get it!'), discuss the findings of the research project, and share the draft of the book with the students.

On behalf of the team, I thank you in advance for participating in this exciting project.

Waldemar Schmidt

Attached: Our research questionnaire

RESEARCH QUESTIONNAIRE

FROM MBA TO CEO (CAREER PLANNING AND DEVELOPMENT FROM A–Z)

Why I decided to do my MBA and what I expect to get out of it:

_____

My dream job is to become:

❑ CEO	❑ Investment banker
❑ Entrepreneur	❑ Managing Partner Professional Firm
❑ Private Equity	❑ Other:
❑ Consultant	❑ Not yet decided

Please list your three burning questions (in order of priority if possible) to the five subjects below:

1. The job of the CEO?

_____

_____

2. Planning of a career that can lead me to my dream job as a CEO:

_____

_____

3. How to keep developing my career once I have stepped on to the CEO career ladder?

_____

_____

4. I would like some good advice regarding the following leadership challenges, which I believe that I will face on my way to the CEO job:

_____

_____

5. I suggest that you also consider the following for the book:

_____

_____

Name/nationality: _____

MBA Class/Business school: _____

Email address: _____

Do you want your name to be listed in the book? ❑ Yes ❑ No

Date: _____

PARTICIPATING MBA BUSINESS SCHOOLS AND STUDENTS

Approximately 200 students from 10 leading business schools have participated in our project. They come from 25 different countries and have either filled in our research questionnaire and/or attended our lecture, 'The job of the CEO... and how you get it'. Some accepted our offer of having their names printed in the book. We take this opportunity to thank all for their effort, time and enthusiasm. Your help has made it possible to write a book that addresses the very specific questions that you and many other ambitious young executives have raised.

PARTICIPATING BUSINESS SCHOOLS:

China Europe International Business School (CEIBS), Shanghai, China

Copenhagen Business School (CBS), Denmark

Fundacao Getulio Vargas, Sao Paulo, Brazil

Guanghua School of Management, Peking University (GSM), China

Hong Kong University of Science & Technology, Business School (HKUST), Hong Kong

Indian School of Business (ISB), Hyderabad, India

International Institute for Management Development (IMD), Lausanne, Switzerland

London Business School (LBS), UK

SKOLKOVO Moscow School of Management, Russia

University of Cape Town, Graduate School of Business (UCT/GBS), South Africa

PARTICIPATING MBA STUDENTS:

200 students have participated in the research project of which the below have accepted to have their name listed:

Abhishek Saraf (ISB), India
Adeel Hyder (LBS), UK, Pakistan & Oman
Aidine Hoek (IMD), The Netherlands
Aileen Fang (CBS), Philippines & USA
Ali Kheloui (IMD), France & Algeria
Aline Hochman (LBS), Brazil
Amanda Lei (CEIBS) China
Anchiet Goel (CEIBS), India
Andrey Korovkin (SKOLKOVO), Russia
Andrey Pchelintsev (SKOLKOVO), Russia
Anna Voss (CBS), Germany

Anthony Hope (HKUST), UK
Arjun Nair (SKOLKOVO), India
Ayesha Fuller (LBS), UK
Brian Chen (IMD), Taiwan & Canada
Brian McMahon (CEIBS), USA
Carlos Conde (CEIBS), Spain
Carol Zhang (CEIBS), China
Carolyn Tiet (CEIBS), Australia/China
Chris Rice (LBS), UK and USA
Christian Kircher (IMD), Mexico & Germany
Clarke Schaumann (CEIBS), USA
Dale Ellsworth Sherrow III (CBS), USA
Damir Samigullin (SKOLKOVO), Russia
Daniel Ambrosio (LBS), USA
Daniel Cerejido (SKOLKOVO), Spain
Daniel Choi (CEIBS), Philippines
Daniela da Silva (CBS), Portugal
David Basson (IMD), UK
Dominique Straessler (CEIBS), Switzerland
Erik Xu (CEIBS), China
Evgeny Raguzin (SKOLKOVO), Russia
Francisco Villegas (SKOLKOVO), Peru
Freddy Baetting (IMD), Switzerland
Frederik Madsen (IMD), Denmark
Galina Antova (IMD), Bulgaria & Canada
Giho Jeong (CEIBS), Korea
Hazem Ragab (CBS), Egypt
Ingvar Jonsson (CBS), Iceland
Jaimin Sibal (SKOLKOVO), India
Jean-David Kirassian (IMD), France
Jericson Co (CEIBS), Canada
Jin Wan (CEIBS), China
Joanne Lau Sze Ki (HKUST), Hong Kong
Johannes Kircher (CEIBS), Germany

Kamina Aisola (IMD), The Netherlands & India
Kathyayani Babbiti (ISB), India
Kay Maenner (CBS), Germany
Kemi Owonubi (IMD), Nigeria
Kevin Millan Uribe (LBS), Mexico
Ksenia Ageeva (SKOLKOVO), Russia
Lani Pollworth (CBS), USA
Leoné Margaret Nowell (CBS), UK and South Africa
Lieven Caboor (LBS), Belgium
Lijun (Julie) Zhu (CEIBS), China
Lochner Joubert (UCT/GSB), South Africa
Lode Van Laere (LBS), Belgium
Maia Matshikiza (CBS), South Africa
Manoel Queiros Ferreira (LBS), Brazil
Marc van Rooijen (IMD), The Netherlands
Marcel Luts (CBS), Germany
Marco Solis (CBS), Chile
Marcus Alves (SKOLKOVO), Brazil
Marko Wolther (IMD), Germany
Maryam Kazemieh (CBS), USA
Matthijs Gille (IMD), The Netherlands
Michael Conry (IMD), Ireland
Mina S. W. Mousa (SKOLKOVO), Egypt.
Mounir Mouawad (LBS), Lebanon
Muzaffar Buhari (IMD), Pakistan
Nipun Jain (ISB), India
Patrick Manasse (SKOLKOVO), USA/Germany
Patrick Manesis (LBS), Greece & Ireland
Patrick Schneider-Sikorsky (SKOLKOVO), UK
Pavel Popikov (IMD), Russia
Philippe Lenssen (SKOLKOVO), Belgium
Phoebe Poon (CBS), Singapore
Pooya Nikooyeh (LBS), Iran/Australia
Pratik Sabherwal (CEIBS), India

Quillan Tang (CEIBS), China
Rahul Bagde (CEIBS), India
Robert Eric Brown (SKOLKOVO), United Kingdom
Roberto Cerdeira (LBS), Brazil
Roslyn Chua (CEIBS), Philippines
Rucsandra Ana Maria Tipa (CBS), USA and Romania
Ryota Yamada (CEIBS), Japan
Sadaf Zahid (LBS), Pakistan
Samuel Galbois (LBS), France
Sanjar Ibragimov (IMD), Uzbekistan
Saori Nishida (IMD), Japan
Sharan Pasricha (LBS), UK/India
Shrini Rawindran (ISB), India
Stepan Kolesnichenko (SKOLKOVO), Russia
Sven Fleischer (CBS), Germany
Svenja Mintert (CBS), Germany
Tak Lo (LBS), Hong Kong
Tina Li (CEIBS), China
Trisha Tan (LBS), Philippines
Varun Dinodiya (LBS), India
Weilin Fan (GSM). China
Zhao Yang (GSM), China
Zhigang Pan (CBS), China

EGON ZEHNDER

EGON ZEHNDER (www.egonzehnder.com) was founded in 1964 with a distinctive vision and structure aimed at achieving two basic goals: to place our clients' interests first and to lead our profession in creating value for our clients through the assessment and recruitment of top-level management resources.

The most fundamental expression of our client-first vision resides in our structure, which is unique to our profession. Our 390 consultants, operating from 63 wholly owned offices in 37 countries, are organised around a single-profit centre partnership. This is designed to eliminate competitive barriers between our offices. It allows us to operate seamlessly when engagements call for us to mobilize across many offices in a country or a region.

Large or small, local or global, our clients benefit from our structure by having access to our most relevant resources and relationships wherever they may reside.

Underpinning this unique structure is our private ownership. We have chosen to operate our firm independent of any outside interests and are motivated solely by a desire to exceed our clients' expectations.

ACKNOWLEDGEMENTS

As mentioned in the introduction, this book is the result of great teamwork.

A big thank you goes to Janet Shaner, MBA Director at IMD; Michala Roeder, Programme Manager at CBS; Cathy Youthed, Global Advisory Council Manager at LBS; Stephan Dertnig, MBA Director at Skolkovo; Nain Segram, MBA Director at GSB, University of Cape Town; Dongxia Wang, Director of the Career Development Centre at Guanghua School of Management, Peking University; Judy Qu, Manager at EIBS; Juni Ip, Manager of Student Development, MBA Programme at HKUST Business School and Deepak Chandra, Deputy Dean at ISB. These individuals and their colleagues very kindly facilitated our interaction with the MBA students for the research project and our lectures. Needless to say, their assistance has been of the utmost importance.

Another big thank you goes to the partners at Egon Zehnder who co-lectured with me and supported me throughout the course of this project. I have been both client and candidate with Egon Zehnder for over 25 years, and also have co-operated with them when penning *Winning at Service—Lessons from Service Leaders*. Our many years of cooperation have proven to be very valuable when writing *From MBA to CEO*.

Apax Foundation kindly contributed to our project, and we are very grateful for their generous contribution.

ABOUT THE AUTHOR

WALDEMAR SCHMIDT is probably best known as a former CEO of ISS—the Copenhagen-based facility services group that is amongst the ten largest corporate employers in the world.

During his long career at ISS, Waldemar held positions from Country Manager in Brazil to CEO of the global group.

Since 2000, Waldemar Schmidt has pursued a new full-time career, holding a variety of positions, including chairmanships and directorships of international companies in six different countries. He is also a prolific writer and lecturer, and is an adjunct professor of strategy and service leadership at Copenhagen Business School.

Between 2001 and 2003, he was an executive-in-residence at IMD in Switzerland where he undertook a research project that resulted in his first book, *Winning at Service*. His second book, *Denmark Limited, Global by Design*, explored the way in which Denmark became one of the world's most competitive nations. He is also co-author of *The Nørby Report*—a study commissioned by the Danish government to establish guidelines for good corporate governance.

Whilst managing ISS's business in Brazil, he received the Export Oscar from the Danish Foreign Ministry. In 2000, the Queen of Denmark awarded Waldemar Schmidt the Order of the Knight of Dannebrog and promoted him to Knight of Dannebrog 1st Degree in 2008. In 2006, he was awarded the Order of the Polar Star by King Carl XVI Gustaf of Sweden.

Made in the USA
Lexington, KY
18 July 2014